WHAT REMAINS OF THE OLD TESTAMENT

WHAT REMAINS OF THE OLD TESTAMENT
AND OTHER ESSAYS

BY

HERMANN GUNKEL

Translated by
THE REV. A. K. DALLAS, M.A.

WIPF & STOCK · Eugene, Oregon

Wipf and Stock Publishers
199 W 8th Ave, Suite 3
Eugene, OR 97401

What Remains of the Old Testament and Other Essays
By Gunkel, Hermann and Dallas, A. K.
ISBN 13: 978-1-60608-514-1
Publication date 3/1/2016
Previously published by Macmillan, 1928

DEDICATED

TO THE

SOCIETY OF BIBLICAL LITERATURE AND EXEGESIS,
NEW YORK,

AS A TOKEN OF RESPECT

AND OF GRATITUDE

FOR THE HONOUR BESTOWED BY THEM ON
THE AUTHOR.

HALLE, *May* 1927

PREFACE

BY

Rev. Professor JAMES MOFFATT, D.D.,
New York

THE five studies which Mr. Dallas has chosen and translated in this book are all devoted to the Old Testament. Yet Professor Gunkel's first work was in the field of the New Testament; as far back as 1888 he published a remarkable monograph on *Die Wirkungen des heiligen Geistes*, which dealt with the experiences of the Spirit in the primitive Christian communities, and he has also contributed a commentary on the First Epistle of St. Peter to the *Schriften* series, edited by Johannes Weiss. At the same time, his main work has been done in Old Testament criticism, where his reputation shines high. No one who has endeavoured to penetrate into the realities of Old Testament religion will fail to acknowledge the debt he owes to books like Gunkel's commentaries upon Genesis and the Psalms, for example. They possess the rare combination of learning and vision. The literary criticism is accompanied by a religious sympathy, which is a constant refreshment to the mind. For Professor Gunkel's two main interests are these: the setting of the Old Testament in the larger context of ancient Oriental civilization, and the connection of the Hebrew religion with the actual experience of the people. In both departments he has been a pioneer, and in both his historical imagination and spiritual intuitions have been richly displayed.

It is astonishing and regrettable that his work has not been made accessible to English readers. Some German theological writers fail to win this entrance; Rothe is a case in point. Gunkel, in our own day, is another. But I feel confident that those who have read these studies will recognize that their author has something incisive to say which few other Old Testament scholars in Germany are able to contribute. Kazlitt used to draw a distinction between Sir James Mackintosh and Coleridge by saying that while "the first knows all that has been said on a subject, the last has something to say that was never said before." Professor Gunkel belongs to the second class. And even when others have said what he says, there is a quality of imagination and intuition in his writing which is too uncommon to be missed. No Old Testament critic of our age is more suggestive. None appreciate more truly the value of the Old Testament as a religious classic. The studies in this volume display him as a keen literary critic and also as a man of genuine moral and spiritual insight. His introduction to an English audience is long overdue, but I hope and believe that these characteristic essays from his pen will not only extend his reputation in circles beyond Germany, but also promote what has been one of his chief ends in life, the better appreciation of the faith that throbs within the tales and songs and prophecies of Old Testament literature.

JAMES MOFFATT.

CONTENTS

		PAGE
PREFACE		9

CHAPTER
I.	WHAT IS LEFT OF THE OLD TESTAMENT?	13
II.	FUNDAMENTAL PROBLEMS OF HEBREW LITERARY HISTORY	57
III.	THE RELIGION OF THE PSALMS	69
IV.	THE CLOSE OF MICAH	115
V.	JACOB	151
	INDEX	187

WHAT REMAINS OF THE OLD TESTAMENT

I

WHAT IS LEFT OF THE OLD TESTAMENT?[1]

A taste for the Old Testament is a touchstone for " Great " and " Small."—NIETZSCHE.

THIS question takes for granted that much of the Old Testament which was a matter of faith for past generations has ceased to hold that position in our minds, and that we are neither able nor anxious to retain all that our forefathers thought they possessed in the Old Testament. Let us begin by asking how this change has taken place, how it has come about that the Old Testament appears to the present generation in another light than that in which it appeared to our forefathers.

When the Christian Church came into existence it accepted not only the Old Testament writings, but also the doctrine that that book was a work of God Himself, given and inspired by the Holy Ghost. Although in the course of the first Christian centuries the New Testament came to occupy a place alongside the Old, the esteem in which the Old Testament was held continued as before, and both collections were handed down through almost two thousand years, both equally

[1] First printed in *Die Deutsche Rundschau*, xli, 1914, and published separately by Vandenhoek und Ruprecht, Göttingen, 1916.

accepted as the Word of God and as the source of true doctrine; every sentence, nay, every letter, being received as divine and infallible. This unqualified estimate of the Old Testament continued almost unchanged down to the middle of the eighteenth century, and, although it has lost some of its uncompromising definiteness, it is by no means extinct even now. But Bible Science, which came into existence about the middle of the eighteenth century, and gradually gathered strength and confidence, first challenged that view, then attacked it, and finally shook it to its foundations, if it has not completely destroyed it.

Many of the positions which Old Testament Science has examined have gradually become familiar to all, but a few of them may be here briefly indicated.

Many of the traditions with regard to the authors of the Old Testament writings which have come down to us—either in the Bible itself, in the form of titles and superscriptions, or from sources outside of the Bible—have been proved to be erroneous. Thus only certain passages in the book of Isaiah are from the hand of that ancient prophet. The book of Daniel does not belong to the Babylonian Exile, but to a much later period. The book of Proverbs was not written by Solomon, neither was Ecclesiastes, nor The Song of Songs. The Psalms which are called by David's name were not all written by that king; indeed, it is questionable whether one single Psalm is Davidic. Again, the idea that the first five books of the Bible are the work of Moses was a mistake of tradition. As a matter of fact, these books were not written by any one single author, but are a collection of ancient writings gradually put together. These ancient writings themselves belong to various periods, and the mere raising of the question whether

WHAT IS LEFT OF THE OLD TESTAMENT?

they are Mosaic is conceivable only in the case of very few of them. These positions are nowadays regarded as common ground by all workers in the sphere of Old Testament Science, and accepted even by conservative scholars.

Again, doubt has been cast on the credibility of many of the Biblical *narratives*. Natural Science has long recognized that the sequence of the works of Creation, as given in the opening chapters of Genesis, is entirely out of keeping with modern views: e.g. the Biblical account places the creation of plant life before that of the heavenly bodies. To us it seems puerile to believe that Elisha on one occasion caused an iron axe-head to float on the water. A modern reader smiles when he finds it recorded as an historical fact that a she-ass opened its mouth and spoke, or that a man spent three days in the belly of a great fish and thereafter emerged alive, or that the first human beings lived for centuries.

Once more, there are numerous *contradictory statements* in the Old Testament. How, for example, could Cain marry a wife and build a city at a time when there were no human beings in the world?

When observations of this kind had once shaken the esteem in which the Old Testament was held, people gained courage to go farther and give expression to criticisms regarding the *religion* and the *morality* of the Old Testament. And, indeed, there is much in it that cannot but offend—sometimes very gravely—a pure, unperverted feeling. Jacob, by lies and deception, obtains the divine blessing. Some have tried to read into this narrative the idea of a divine discipline and a conversion of the deceiver, but the narrative itself does not contain one single word that indicates disapproval of the deception he practised on Isaac. In Egypt,

Abraham passes his wife off as his sister, and it is only by divine interposition that the matter ends without evil result. Again, surprise is felt at the exclusive nature of the relation in which the religion stands to the nation and the national interests. Jahveh is the God of Israel and of no other people. Israel's wars are (neither more nor less) Jahveh's wars. The pious Hebrew hurls fearful curses against the enemy of his nation without any feeling of the injustice and wrong involved in such conduct:

> Blessed is he who takes and dashes
> Thy children against the rocks.

The book of Esther, which espouses with a blind bigotry the cause of the Jews against the Gentiles, cannot be read by a Christian or a non-Jew without great distaste, such as that to which Luther gave candid expression. Professor Paulsen, the philosopher, a man of deep piety and great nobility of character, whose incorruptible opinion is entitled to claim a hearing from everyone, once expressed to me his horror at the terrible wholesale murders recorded in the book of Joshua, deeds of blood which are rendered hardly more tolerable by the thought that they were committed only on paper and not in reality. Thus the opinion that the Old Testament is a safe guide to true religion and morality cannot any longer be maintained.

In view of all this, it is not surprising that during last century a vigorous discussion was carried on with reference to these and numerous similar "causes of offence" in the Old Testament. The opponents of religion and of the Bible seized on them as subjects of mockery. Lovers of the Bible, on the other hand, too often saw, in the criticisms urged by Bible-loving

WHAT IS LEFT OF THE OLD TESTAMENT? 17

scholars, nothing but the results of unbelief. Another serious hindrance to a proper understanding of the Old Testament was the fact that many unthinking people identified ancient Israel with the Jews of our own day, leaving out of account the long interval between the ancient past and the present time, and forgetting that the great changes that have passed upon Israel in the course of three thousand years cannot possibly have been without effect on the national character of that people. This is just as intelligent as it would be to see a typical representative of the ancient Germans in a German commercial traveller of to-day. Again, many half-informed people, unable to forget their former estimate of the Old Testament, find themselves unable to read its writings simply as human works. Their historical education is in many cases good enough to enable them to appreciate the differences between the Old Testament and the New, but it is not comprehensive enough to enable them to study such an ancient book simply and without prejudice. People of this kind take offence at incidents narrated in the Old Testament which would be quite inoffensive if they occurred, say, in Homer. They feel hurt when they read about Jacob's deceit, but they can read with pleasure about the constant lying of Odysseus. If they could only bring themselves to understand the Hebrew narrative simply as a roguish piece of folk-lore, that is to say, if they would read it in the sense in which it was originally meant, they would see it in an entirely different light.

It is an open secret that in this regard the position of elementary school teachers in Germany has been specially difficult. In the Training Colleges they received an obsolete conception of the Bible, and later in life they have not been able to exclude from their minds thoughts and feelings such as those we have mentioned. Being required, however, to give instruction in the Old Testament, without themselves having had any comprehensive or detailed guidance how the newer conceptions are to be presented to children, they find their work a heavy burden, and there need be no surprise when the cry is raised, "The Old Testament should be abolished from the elementary schools. Are we justified in introducing Christian children to the sacred book of the Jews?" And it is not only teachers who are asking this question. The Bible-Babel controversy has revealed how many people have felt the force of the criticisms that have been directed against the Old Testament, and who, when they learn that parts of the Old Testament are of Babylonian origin, are ready to throw the whole book overboard. Whoever pays attention to what is being thought and said in our day cannot fail to hear the eagerness with which the question is asked, "What is left to us of the Old Testament?"

To this question Old Testament Science is prepared to give a frank and clear reply. For a century and a half scholars have been busy, first groping uncertainly, then progressing with increasing confidence, till they have now worked out a clear conception of what the Old Testament is. Among the scholars who have helped to achieve this result Julius Wellhausen will always be named with honour. Old Testament scholarship, by means of great acumen, patient detailed investigation, and a power of intuition amounting to genius, has sketched a splendid picture of the history of the people of Israel, its religion and its literature. In so doing it has definitively given up the *old* conception of Inspiration. To Old Testament Science the Bible is in the first instance a book produced by human means in human ways. Science has brought it down from heaven and set it up in the midst of the earth. It treats the Old Testament and the people of Israel with the same methods as would be applied to any other book and any other people. And by doing so Old Testament Science justly claims to be a fully qualified member of the circle of historical Sciences. A University which gives no place to this Science cannot claim to be in a full sense a *universitas literarum*. Just because we have dealt with the Old Testament in this manner, we have rediscovered its true significance for the history of the world; and to the question, "What do we have in the Old Testament?" we reply, soberly and definitely: "We have a great treasure, a very great treasure, in the Old Testament."

To begin with, we have in the Old Testament *an almost illimitable wealth of artistic stimulation*. It was one of the German classical writers [1] who discovered the beauty of the Old Testament, and Goethe, who, like Bacon, "took all knowledge for his province," followed that discovery with sympathy and interest. In his notes to the *Westöstlichen Divan*, he writes: "When we recall the time when Herder and Eichhorn pointed this out to us, we are reminded of a great delight comparable to a veritable Oriental sunrise." In the Prologue to his greatest poem, Goethe had in mind the Prologue to the book of Job; and in the concluding act of the second part of the same poem, where angels and devils fight for Faust's soul, we have an echo of a Jewish legend, in which a similar fight takes place for the dead body of Moses, so that a brilliant writer of modern days has even called Moses both the prototype and antitype of Faust.[2] Everyone knows also how devotedly Goethe

[1] Herder [Translator].   [2] Burdach, *Faust und Moses*, 1912.

WHAT REMAINS OF THE OLD TESTAMENT

from early youth read the Old Testament, how greedily he drank in Luther's glorious translation, and how, by making his own Luther's powerful Bible German, he invigorated the German literary language of his time, which had degenerated to insipidity. Our educated people, even our lovers of æsthetics, seem to have forgotten what living streams of poetical beauty are found in the Old Testament. Our pious people are wont to say that the Bible walks abroad in the guise of a slave, wearing the humble garments of a beggar. To be sure, by no means everything in the Old Testament is of equal æsthetic value; there is much in it that is, from this point of view, arid and desolate enough. But looking at it as a whole we may nevertheless say that the Old Testament wears no beggar's dress, but the royal robe that befits it.

In the first place, among the best known æsthetic creations of the Bible are those glorious *poetical narratives*, of marvellous insight and unique feeling for beauty of form, composed with truly classical sense of style, and therefore the delight of artists down through the ages and the theme of ever new creations, imitated again and again, in poetry and on canvas—narratives which bring the life of early days vividly before our eyes, a well of rejuvenescence for a civilization grown old, intelligible at sight to our children, beloved by them, and embodying for them lofty and eternal thoughts. Think of the force with which, in the Cain story, murder is set forth as the basal crime; the charm of the Joseph story, eloquent of fraternal envy and fraternal love, and full of faith in an overruling Providence; the attractiveness of the Ruth idyl, exhibiting a widow's love lasting beyond death and the grave; the magnificent solemnity of the Creation narrative; the wondrous

WHAT IS LEFT OF THE OLD TESTAMENT? 21

story of Paradise, naïve yet profound. Old Testament Science has only begun to apply itself to the study of this æsthetic side of the narratives. One should imagine that philologists, historians of civilization, and all interested in æsthetics would vie with us in holding up to view these golden treasures, and that even our poets would study these ancient narratives and learn from them the secret of compact power, unity of construction, and graphic clearness. We hope this will ere long be the case. Meantime, however, we would say to teachers: Realize what valuable material you have in these narratives. How much poorer in poetical materials our schools would be if these were absent from them! Nay, it would mean ruin to our æsthetic civilization if adults, not having learned the Old Testament at school, should be unable to understand at once allusions to those Old Testament narratives which former times have bequeathed to us in lavish abundance.

Again, there are the prophets—many of them also poets of the first rank, using a language full of power and energy and majestic elevation—trumpets of God, uttering notes of such strength that our ears can hardly bear them, filled with overwhelming anger and overflowing with rapture, or at other times melting into pity, torn by grief and sorrow, and withal rising to defiant faith. Here, too, is a marvellously varied world —only partially, it is true, intelligible to our children— unlike any modern literature, but just because of its strangeness, its bizarre, rugged greatness, full of attractiveness to our older pupils. And in this poetical dress, which no one who has known it can ever forget, we have the highest thoughts of the human race; above all, the imperishable power of the Moral Idea.

Let us look at a few passages in order to gain some

idea of the poetic power of the prophets. Take first the famous passage of Isaiah, in which he describes the approach of dread Assyria.[1] Summoned by Jahveh Himself—a thought both sublime and terrible to the Israelite of that time—Assyria advances from the end of the earth, marching with unresting haste. No obstacle, such as usually delays an army's advance, stops its course. With his terrible war-cry, like the roar of a lion making his adversary quake, he springs upon Israel, and then stands shrieking over his prey. An obscure image, borrowed from the ancient Creation-myth, concludes the dreadful description—darkness covers heaven and earth, and through the darkness sounds the roar of the enemy, like the roaring of the raging sea. Primeval chaos—darkness and great waters—again prevails; the last fight and end of the old Germanic gods, as we should say, has come:

> He raises a banner 'for the people from afar'[2]
>   and hisses it on from the end of the earth:
>   it comes hasting on, at full speed!
> No stumbler, no tired man amongst them!
>   It needs neither slumber nor sleep!
> The girdle of its loins is not loosed,
>   the thong of its shoes is not broken.
> Its arrows remain sharp,
>   its bows are all bent.
> The hoofs of its steeds
>   are like to the flint,
>   its wheels like the storm.
> It raises a roar like the lion,
>   it roars like the young lion and howls,
> and seizes the prey and bears it away
>   and there is none who can save.

[1] Is. v. 26–30.
[2] Alterations in the text are shown by ' '. For the text cf. Kittel's *Biblia Hebraica*.

> It howls over it
> on that day
> like sea roaring.
> If one looks to the earth—distressful darkness,
> 'and' the light grew dark in the clouds.[1]

Among all the battle scenes which the Assyrians and Egyptians have left us, there is not one that can compare in vivid grandeur with this Old Testament picture.

Take another passage of the same prophet, describing the end of the Assyrian dominion and the coming of the Messiah.[2] In a time of misery, due to foreign oppression, the prophet sees his people walking in "the land of darkness," that is, in the land where the sun is unknown—a legendary idea that also appears elsewhere. But he also sees the hour of deliverance, when the sheen of the glorious light pierces into this awesome land. That will be a day of rejoicing, of rejoicing like that of the harvest-time, or like that of the people dividing the booty brought home at the end of a war. What means this light? Why this joy? The prophet explains it in a parable. Up till now Israel was like a beast of burden, sighing under the heavy oppression of Assyria; now Jahveh has broken the yoke and destroyed the oppressor's rods. Then a new image rises before the prophet's eye: the enemy's army is destroyed; the battlefield is strewn with the weapons of the enemy, cast away in his sudden flight. These are all gathered into a great heap, and what till now was Israel's terror is burned in the fire—the war boots in which the enemy had once marched with the noise of thunder, and the martial cloaks stained with the blood of the slain. Then the prophet's eye passes from the deliverance to the deliverer. A new ruler appears in Israel, a mysterious

---

[1] The last word is doubtful. [2] Is. ix. 2–7.

child, bearing on his shoulder the rod of a prince. And by means of a series of Divine names the prophet announces what the characteristics of this new ruler will be. Wise in counsel, never at a loss, he will be "wonderful," and in his strength he will be like to a god. Like a father he will guard his people for ever and give them the peace they long for. Thus on David's ancient throne—for the Wonderful One is of David's line—there will arise the dominion of righteousness and peace for ever. But all this is due to the "zeal" of Jahveh Zebaoth, who will not allow His people to be robbed or harmed by the heathen.

> The people, who are walking in darkness,
>   saw a great light :
> Those who dwelt in the dark land,
>   'Glory'[1] shines upon them !
> Thou bringest great 'rejoicing'   and great exultation
>   they rejoice before thee   as with harvest joy,
>   as men rejoice,   when they divide the spoil.
> For the yoke of his burden,   'the staff' of his neck' '
>   hast thou as on Midian's day[2] broken !
> For every war boot that strode along noisily,
>   Every robe, 'stained' with blood,
> they were burned,   they were food for the fire !
>   For a scion has arisen for us,
>   a son given to us,
> who bears on his shoulder dominion,
>   and his name is :
> Marvel in counsel,   a God of a hero,
>   Father for ever,   prince of peace.
> 'Great is righteousness'[3] and peace without end
>   on David's seat   and in his realm :
> he bases it firmly[4]
>   on justice and righteousness
>   from henceforth for ever !
> Jahveh Zebaoth's   zeal accomplishes it !

[1] The Hebrew text must have had a different word here.
[2] That is, on the day when Midian was defeated by Gideon in the time of the Judges.   [3] rab hammīsōr.   [4] laḥᵃchināh.

No one who looks fairly at such pictures can ever lose the impression made by these strong colours. Surely it is high time that men should awake from their neglect of the prophetical writings.

In the third place there is the whole realm of *Old Testament lyric poetry*, containing secular and spiritual poems of the most varied kind. Like the prophetic writings, these are not all of equal worth, but they include many of the most fascinating and delightful creations in all literature, some with a deep organ tone and some undulating and rippling like the sea. But better than any description will be a few examples.

In imperishable words, full of deep sadness, the Psalmist sings of the brevity and misery of human life: he does not, however, in his sorrow, sink into impotence, but sets over against this human fate the eternity of God, immeasurable by any human gauge: men pass away, but God abides.[1]

> ' Jahveh ' ' ' Thou abidest for ever God,
>   ' ' ' and from of old hast Thou been, ' '
> ere mountains were brought forth,
>   ere earth and world revolved.
> For a thousand years are before Thee
>   like yesterday's day, when ' they are past.'
>
> Thou bringest men to ' their ' dust again
>   ' and ' sayst: Return, ye children of men.
> ' ' Only a watch in the night ' thou appointest ' :
>   ' When they are relieved, they fall on sleep.'
>
> ' ' Like the grass, ' ' that blooms in the morning, ' '
>   in the evening it fades and withers,
> ' Thus ' we vanish by Thy anger,
>   we are scared away by Thy wrath.

---

[1] Ps. xc. 2*c*, 1*b*, 2*a b*, 4*a b*, 3, 4*c*, 5, 6, 7. For the texts cf. my *Ausgewählte Psalmen* and my *Commentary on the Psalms*.

Or take the following passage from the profound Ps. cxxxix. 7-12 :

> Whither shall I go from Thy Spirit,
>   whither flee from Thy presence ?
> Mount I to heaven, Thou art there !
>   take I hell for my bed, there too Thou art !
>
> If I rose on the wings of the rose of dawn,
>   alighted at the end of the sea :
> there too would Thy hand ' seize ' me,
>   Thy right hand grasp me.
>
> If I ' said ' : Let darkness sheer ' cover me,'
>   and night me all round ' enclose,'
> even darkness were not for Thee darkness,
>   and night would shine clear like the day.' '

Or, once more, Ps. cxxxvii, a poem full of pain and home-sickness, with a savage close :

> By Babel's streams
>   there we sat down and wept,
>   when we remembered Zion.
> On the poplar-trees there we hung up
>   our harps.
>
> For there our ravishers desired from us
>   strains of melody,
>   and our ' pillagers ' mirth :
> " Sing ye to us one
>   of Zion's songs."
>
> How could we sing Jahveh's songs
>   on foreign soil !
> If I forget thee, Jerusalem,
>   then may my right hand ' fail ' !
>
> May my tongue cleave to my palate
>   if I think no more of thee,
> if I set not Jerusalem
>   above my chiefest joy !

> Remember, Jahveh,
>   Edom's sons,
>   on the day of Jerusalem!
> They said: Tear down, tear down,
>   down to the ground!
>
> Daughter of Babel, thou 'murderess,'
>   Blessed is he who pays thee home ' '!
> Blessed is he who takes and dashes
>   thy children on the rock!

This poem tells us how keen foreigners were to enjoy the strains of a Hebrew melody. We may infer that even in ancient times Hebrew music was renowned throughout the world. This inference is supported by the fact that King Hezekiah was compelled to deliver his musical instruments to the Assyrians along with other valuables. We of the present day, who are now beginning to know the poetry of Babylon, Assyria, and Egypt, cannot but confirm this verdict of the ancient world. Taken as a whole, all the poetry of the ancient East is much inferior to that of the Hebrews, and the highest praise that can be given to a Babylonian or Egyptian song is that it is not altogether unworthy of being compared with the poems in the Bible. And what a wealth of varied forms is set before us here! The Hebrew poets describe in triumphant strains the majesty of Jahveh. They celebrate His glory in Creation: "The heavens declare the glory of the Eternal"; His forgiving grace to Israel: "As a father pitieth his children, so the Lord pitieth them that fear Him." Or they lament with hearts broken by their personal sorrow or by national misfortune, or from their tears they look up confidently to God. Perhaps the most arresting, because the most genuine of all their poems, are those in which in liturgical fashion alternate voices are heard, in which at first, with bell-like tones, the confidence of their faith is strongly expressed, and then the note of pain of the burdened heart is heard—the burdened heart that yearns for those heights of bliss.

Take as an example Ps. lxxxv. In the lofty tone of prophetic vision the first part announces as present actual fact the salvation that is still to come:

> Thou hast, O Jahveh, favoured Thy land,
>   hast turned the fate of Jacob,
> hast remitted the guilt of Thy people,
>   forgiven all ' their sins ' :
> hast recalled all Thine anger,
>   and quenched the ' fire ' of Thy wrath.

The second part contains a prayer, expressing the yearning of the people for this salvation:

> Restore Thou us, O God of help,
>   ' let ' Thy displeasure against us ' cease ' !
> Wilt Thou be angry with us always ?
>   and prolong Thine anger for ever ?
> Wilt ' ' Thou not quicken us again,
>   that Thy people may rejoice in Thee ?
> Let us, O Jahveh, Thy mercy see
>   and grant us Thy salvation !

The third stanza reverts to the opening note. Out of the circle of singers rises a man accustomed to hear the Divine voice. And he is able to announce that what the downcast hearts so ardently desire is at hand ! Salvation is near !

> I will listen to what ' ' Jahveh will speak,
>   Verily, He speaks of salvation
> to His people and to His faithful ones,
> ' and, to those who turn to Him, of hope.'
> Yea, near is His aid to His pious ones,
>   that His glory may dwell in our land.

WHAT IS LEFT OF THE OLD TESTAMENT? 29

> Mercy and truth meet,
>   Righteousness and peace kiss ' each other.'
> Truth sprouts out of the earth,
>   Grace looks down from heaven.
> Jahveh Himself gives all that is good,
>   Our land yields its fruit.
> Grace goes before Him,
>   and ' straightness ' on the path of His steps.

Thus ends the poem in a tone of ecstatic vision: Salvation and Grace on all sides, above and beneath, and everywhere.

Songs like these cry for a composer. They were once meant to be sung; they ought to be set to music once more. Would not Bach have known how to do justice to the varied religious moods of these songs if he had known them in their newer, more vivid interpretation?

Speaking generally, the Hebrew mind had not the type of genius required for lengthy productions, and so the shorter the pieces the more beautiful they are. The Hebrew had a special gift for painting a richly coloured picture in very small compass. But the Hebrew mind succeeded in producing one great poem which is great also in length. I mean the book of Job. Here the author is bold enough to impugn, and even to attack, the strongest base of the whole Hebrew religion, viz. the doctrine of Divine retribution. Sore at heart and afflicted by a horrible and incurable disease —a fate that flatly contradicted the doctrine ardently believed by all good men—he still refuses to give up his conviction of his own innocence. He enters upon a bitter contest with his pious friends, who find their whole religion in this doctrine, and even ventures to call in question the justice of God Himself. Three friends argue with him, but he overthrows all three, and remains alone on the field. Then he rises, and his words sound like an accusation addressed to heaven in the name of all humanity: "Why? Why?" Now comes forth the Eternal One in person, revealing His Divine Majesty in sublime words to the son of earth. All questioning is hushed: "I lay my hand upon my mouth." The book of Job is like a Titan structure towering up to heaven; but at the close all that is of man fades and only God's greatness remains.

It is significant that the orthodoxy of past centuries revealed no understanding of this pearl of Old Testament poetry, just as in some ecclesiastical circles to-day æsthetic considerations are treated with disdain, or even with displeasure. The false halo surrounding everything in the Old Testament prevented its natural beauties from being enjoyed. But we are deliberately emphasizing this æsthetic side in the hope that the reader who has learned to appreciate the beauty of so many of the Biblical poems will also come to love the thoughts they enshrine.

But it is not only the poetry of the Old Testament that has still a message for us, its *History* is also of outstanding importance. The people of Israel produced not only poetical narratives, but also a highly developed historical literature. Portions of this are preserved for us in 2 Samuel and in scattered passages of the other narrative books. This literature has an amazing objectivity. Owing to this really astounding objectivity the work of the Hebrew historian far surpasses anything produced elsewhere in the ancient East. Only by the great historians among the Greeks has he ever been excelled. "Hebrew civilization," says Eduard Meyer,[1] "alone of all the other (ancient Eastern) civilizations, really stands on the same intellectual level as the Greek."

[1] Ed. Meyer, *Die Israeliten und ihre Nachbarstämme*, p. 486.

WHAT IS LEFT OF THE OLD TESTAMENT? 31

The pictures have been painted in such true colours that Hebrew history, incomplete as our knowledge of it is, is more familiar to us than the history of any other people of the ancient East. Everywhere else in the East the annals of history were written in the service of despots, whereas in Israel there prevailed a spirit of freedom which refused to fall slavishly in the dust before the king, but depicted faithfully both him and his doings. Even the legends provide us with an abundance of historical information, revealing clearly the internal conditions of the nation, its religion, its customs, its laws, and its social relationships.

There are two respects in which these historical narratives, like the poetical narratives already discussed, have a great superiority over all modern literature of the same kind. These are *the simplicity of their conceptions* and their *power of depicting details*. In both respects they are suitable for the child mind, and are therefore eminently serviceable for elementary instruction. They appeal even to our youngest children. The conditions of modern life, especially in large cities, have become so unnatural, so complicated and chaotic, that the modern child, whose only knowledge of running water is derived from water-pipes and who knows artificial light only in the form of incandescent electrical globes, finds it extremely difficult to gain clear and simple conceptions. No words are needed to show how much injury is, or can be, done to the intellectual development of a child by the unthinking acceptance of what he finds around him. In spite of all our technical achievements, a new intellectual barbarism may arise in our midst—indeed, its beginnings are perhaps already visible. That is why the subjects of antiquity, and especially the Old Testament narratives, can render service in our education that nothing else can render. In the Biblical narratives the child reads of the most ancient forms of human activity, of hunters, shepherds, and tillers of the soil. He learns of the compelling force of hunger and its power to set history in motion. But he also learns that, in the life of a people that loves righteousness, there is something more important than eating and drinking, and many similar lessons of great value to-day. It would be a lamentable mistake if our teachers were to allow this marvellous material to be taken out of their hands.

And all this in the magic sheen of the distant East! How the young imagination is stirred when it hears of oases and camels and palm-trees! And in after-days, when the child has grown to manhood, the memory of his parents and the days of his youth are intertwined with memories of the large picture-Bible he loved so dearly. Freiligrath sings:

1.
Thou friend of early childhood,
Thou folio brown with age,
How oft dear hands threw open
For me thy sacred page!
Thy wealth of coloured pictures
Made glad my youthful eyes,
And bore me, play forgotten,
To sunny, Eastern skies.

2.
Thou ope'dst for me the portals
Of distant lands and fair,
A mirror clear and beautiful
Of all that sparkles there!
In thee I saw fair visions,
As o'er thy leaves I bent,
Saw palm and desert camel,
Shepherd and shepherd's tent.

WHAT IS LEFT OF THE OLD TESTAMENT? 33

3.
Abram I saw, and Isaac—
Their plain and simple ways.
The angels hovering o'er them
Throughout their earthly days.
I watched their cattle roaming,
Saw flocks their thirst assuage,
And sat and gazed in wonder
Before thy open page.

Will any man actually suggest that, in order to prevent the impoverishment of our children's minds, modern books of travel should be put in the place of the Bible?

But all the things that we have mentioned are but trifles when compared with the greatest treasure of the Old Testament, viz. *its religious value*. Hebrew religion, it is true, is not simply to be identified with the Christian religion. Indeed, in numerous details and in its profoundest thoughts it is much inferior to it; and the type of exposition that is still to be found in many of our schools, an exposition that seeks to obliterate these differences, is open to many objections and involves many dangers. It is just these numerous points where this inferiority of Old Testament religion and morality is most apparent that force the teacher, who has not appreciated these differences, either to resort to all sorts of artificial interpretation or to present to children the religion of ancient Israel as a perfect Divine revelation. Under such circumstances, either truth is sinned against or religion and morality are degraded. That this latter result is sometimes produced is, unfortunately, a sad fact. How much would we give if the Reformation in Germany were clear of the disgraceful taint of the bigamy of the Landgraf, a taint due to the example of the Hebrew patriarchs! All the same, there is in reality a close connection between the two Testaments. The religion of the New Testament arose on the foundation of the Old Testament Jewish religion, and it cannot be scientifically understood without a knowledge of the latter. It is now acknowledged that other religions also have influenced both pre-Christian Judaism and the Christianity that arose from it. Old Testament Science is just beginning to understand these relations (in particular the influence of the "syncretistic" mystery-religions of that time, in which, under the cover of Hellenism, many Oriental elements became intermingled with it) and to get at the real nature of primitive Christianity. But although these investigations are still far from having reached their goal, it can already be said that Christianity is historically inconceivable without the Old Testament basis. Jesus was born and educated as a Jew, and nourished His spirit on the Old Testament; no trace of Hellenistic influence can be found in Him. And although such influence was undoubtedly present in Paul and John, they too remained Jews in all essential elements. It was within the walls of the synagogue that Christianity spent its earliest days. It only left the synagogue when it was forcibly expelled from it, and to the inheritance which it brought with it from its ancestral home, i.e. the Old Testament, it has clung down through the centuries. In its early days the Christian Church did meet one captivating tempter, Gnosticism, which suggested that it should abandon the Old Testament as the charter of an inferior religion. With good reason, the Church resisted this temptation and clung to its Old Testament, in spite of the serious difficulties presented by the task of interpreting it. This position of the Old Testament in the Christian Church is an historical fact, against which it would be foolish to

WHAT IS LEFT OF THE OLD TESTAMENT? 35

grumble. It is extremely improbable that history will ever retrace its steps in this regard. The interpretation of the Old Testament may change, but the right of the Old Testament to its place in the Church is indisputable. It will be read as Holy Scripture as long as the Church endures, and it is simply a result of unhistorical thinking when the proposal is made that the Church should let the Old Testament go. To the very simplest reader of the Bible it can be made clear that he must not overlook the Old Testament if he desires to understand the New. In numberless passages the New refers to the Old and develops the thoughts contained in it. Who can hope to grasp Paul's thought if he knows nothing of the Law from which Christ has delivered us? Or of Adam, through whom sin came into the world? Or of Abraham, whose faith made him the father of all them that believe? Nay, the very name Christianity is a reminder that the first disciples of Jesus transferred to their Master the greatest name in the Old Testament, the name " Christos," the Messiah. It is, to be sure, undeniable that in Paul there are numerous survivals from the Jewish past which we are fully entitled to lay aside. It is clear, too, that both Jesus and Paul, in their contest with the Jewish legalism of their day, opposed that spirit which is found here and there in the legal parts of the Old Testament, especially in the so-called " Priestly Codex " (a post-exilic source of the Pentateuch); but it is also clear that in the main content of their thoughts—up to a certain point—they are children and descendants of the Old Testament. Thus the reader of the Bible always returns to the Old Testament, and as long as our schools provide religious instruction, they cannot help dealing with the Old for the sake of the New. It is useless to discuss the matter.

History has spoken and the case is decided. The Christian Church—a mighty structure—will unfold its nature in the course of its growth, but it will only change it at the cost of serious convulsions; and one of the foundations of the Church is the Old Testament.

But, apart altogether from its connection with the New Testament and with the Christian Church, the Old Testament possesses many features that give it an outstanding religious value for the present day. Here again there are distinctions to be drawn. There is much in the Old Testament that has no religious value—lists of names and genealogical trees and compositions like the Song of Songs, which is a collection of poems treating of love and marriage, interesting on account of their poetic beauty, but of entirely secular value. There are other things too, which, although they were in bygone days held to be of great religious value, have in the course of the history of religion lost that position. We have already spoken of some of these at the beginning of this essay. The close connection of religion with the Jewish nationality has no meaning for us. The Creation story, valuable as its religious thoughts still are, is for us not actual history. The morality of early Israel differs to a large extent from ours. The intolerance of Hebrew religion towards all other religions—an intolerance that is axiomatic to it, as is evidenced by the words " heathen " and " idols," and which has unfortunately penetrated via Judaism into Christianity and has long held a prominent position in it—has become impossible for men who have learned to attach some value to other religions. An unbiased mind will frankly admit differences like these. Christian orthodoxy and Jewish self-complacency do no service to the cause of the Bible

WHAT IS LEFT OF THE OLD TESTAMENT? 37

when they claim that everything in the Old Testament is equally great and valuable. But just because we frankly give up what cannot be defended, we hope to obtain a hearing when we point out *what is of permanent value in the Old Testament*. For the Old Testament has a wealth of thoughts and conceptions which form the imperishable achievements of the Hebrew spirit. These are not, and never can become, obsolete, for they lie at the root of all modern thinking, whatever attitude men may take up towards Church and religion. Besides, the Old Testament contains conceptions which, although they have now been outgrown in the history of thought, can never be forgotten, because they were necessary stages in the path of evolution; and again, the Old Testament has, among its peculiar thoughts, some which form a valuable counterpoise to certain injurious tendencies of our time.

Of the numerous points to which reference might be made in this connection, a few may be here mentioned. We have already spoken of the *simplicity* of Hebrew thought as mirrored in the ancient sagas. This simplicity is a fundamental feature of Hebrew religion. Thoughts that are at the root of all religious and moral civilization have been rammed like posts into its soil. For example, take the principles of morality as expressed in the *Ten Commandments*, with their majestic and inviolable " Thou shalt." Words like these, with the breath of the primeval world upon them, tower up like giant mountain peaks. Empires disappear; nations pass away; even modern nations and States have no promise of permanence; all external civilization is in constant movement, but foundations like these moral principles abide. Who would dare to take them from our children, because for us they are no longer complete as they stand, but require to be extended and applied?

Again, take the great tenet of *Monotheism*—a tenet which seems so simple that any child should be able to understand it. The Deity is to be conceived as a Unity; but the Hebrew conception is far simpler than that. Jahveh, God of Israel, is the one living and true God; beside this figure, concretely conceived, there is no other. This also is an absolutely inviolable tenet, the root of all higher moral and spiritual religion, and finds an echo in every idealistic view of the world down to the present day.

Another tenet of the Old Testament, equally simple, appearing and reappearing in numberless variations, deals with the *Divine retribution of Good and Evil*. That is a great thought, finding a place even among the Ten Commandments. Although it was all too often externalized in ancient Israel, with the result that Retribution was looked for and found to an undue extent in the outward lot of men, still it remains one of the most important principles of every moral religion and of every higher view of the world—the belief, namely, that the natural and the moral government of the world, however often they seem to be at variance, are not at bottom mutually exclusive; that the course of events in its final purpose serves good and not evil ends; that it is constructive and not destructive; that Retribution is a real thing. To be sure, Christianity knows a higher relation between God and man than that of retributive law, but Christianity merely shifts the thought of Retribution into the second place—it by no means suspends it. " Be not deceived: God is not mocked." Our children understand the message of Retribution far better than they understand that of Redemption, for the latter can only be understood when a man has by long and sore experience learned his own impotence, and it is therefore wise to lead our children by the same path that history has trod.

The prophets carried on a controversy with the people of their time with regard to the question, *Wherein consists true service of God?* The view which they combated was the view common to all antiquity, viz. that the Deity should be worshipped by all manner of holy acts, by sacrifice and ceremonies. But the prophets achieved a fundamentally new conception of religion. God does not require men to obey certain holy customs; He demands the entire life, a piety that is shown in action, moral behaviour. A servant-maid sweeping a room can, as Luther expressed it, be leading a holy life, holier than that lived by the monk in his cell. This great principle, which does away with all action that is merely formal—a principle that is also fundamental in the Protestant Church—finds perfect expression in the prophets. " I desire mercy and not sacrifice." Here Religion and Morality have formed an alliance that shall never be dissolved. We cannot conceive a type of piety which is not at the same time moral. To-day all views of the world lead up to morality, even those in which it is not easy to see any relation to morality at all. But in this inward necessity, to which even the modern spirit pays homage, we have an achievement of the Hebrew prophets.

The manner in which these men conceived of *Morality* was also of great importance for the history of the world. With trenchant power they hammered into the hearts of their people, and, through their writings, into the heart of all mankind, the truth that the essence of sin among men is oppression of the lowly, and that righteousness consists in worthy treatment of the poor and the oppressed. When, some decades ago, the economic conditions among modern nations had become intolerable to the masses, this message of the prophets was laid anew on the consciences of men. All modern social legislation is an outcome of the prophetic spirit, and the spirit of these Hebrew teachers will continue to urge the nations to ever fresh reforms.

Further, there is the *Eschatology* of the prophets, their doctrine of the last things. Here, too, the prophets of Israel gave an impulse to the world, the effect of which continues down to our own day. These ardent souls, driven nearly to despair amid the sin and wretchedness of their time, lived on the faith that this world of misery and forgetfulness of God must be followed by a new world in which the ideal will be victorious. This unswerving hope in a better day in store was characteristic of Israel and distinguishes that nation from a people like the Greeks, who knew nothing of such a future hope. This attitude of mind, however, is a fundamental feature of the nations at the present day; all men to-day, however they differ in their ways of thinking, agree in the conviction that the history of humanity is not yet ended. Religious minds are sighing, " It doth not yet appear what we shall be." A modern philosophy is predicting a " superman," and the masses are under the enchantment of the hope of a revolution in economic conditions.

When we try to understand any religion that has appeared, it is of fundamental importance to find out the sphere in which it traces the peculiar workings of God. It is characteristic of the religion of the New Testament that it lays supreme emphasis on the relation of God to men, and that, in comparison with that

WHAT IS LEFT OF THE OLD TESTAMENT? 41

relation, *God's activity in Nature recedes into the background*. Life in and with Nature, such as had existed in bygone days, had, although it was not completely lost, receded into the background. Thus, although the belief that God is at work in Nature was never abandoned in the teaching of the Christian Church—that would have been impossible—it was not specially living or powerful. Since the days of Rousseau and Goethe the deep feeling for Nature has reawakened among modern nations and grown to a degree that was previously undreamt of. If it is rightly guided, this communion with Nature can become an antechamber to the temple of religion. In this regard, therefore, the present day is conscious of a need which cannot be completely satisfied by the New Testament. The Old Testament fills up this gap. In the hymns of Nature contained in the Old Testament, notes are struck which awaken an echo in the hearts of men to-day. Our Churches and our schools should not, as they so often do, continue to pass by these glorious hymns of Nature. We should not be withheld from the study of these poems by the fact that many of them still contain traces of mythological colour; for it is just this peculiar mythological feature, bringing certain phenomena, like the storm, the volcanic eruption, the earthquake, into special and immediate relation to the Deity, that supplies conceptions of outstanding poetic and religious power. The light is " the garment of God "; the heavens are His " tent "; the hills " smoke " when they are " touched by His hand "; to the sea, rushing towards the shore, He sets a limit and says, " Thus far and no farther "; the lions roar to Him for their food, and to the young ravens He gives their nourishment.

There is another aspect in which the Old Testament

can supplement the New. In the New Testament, the actual point where God and man meet is the human heart. The decisive question is, "What must I do to be saved?" The salvation here meant is the salvation of the individual soul, and it is a supramundane, heavenly salvation. Compared with this, the Old Testament is on a lower level, for in its pages religion deals in the first instance with national life, although it was out of this national religion that the higher religion of the individual gradually arose. But at this level of national religion thoughts were born which are still of great value for our time. Chief among these is the thought of the *direct interest of religion in political affairs*. The New Testament, which grew up at a time when the gigantic Roman Empire was endeavouring to wean its provinces from all independent political action and was just about to break the last remnant of Jewish political existence—the only message of the New Testament is subjection to the State. It makes no mention of the duty of positive co-operation in the tasks of the State. There is a different message in the Old Testament, which dates from the time when the Hebrew State was still at its full strength. In the Old Testament we find a magnificent combination of piety and patriotism: "If I forget thee, O Jerusalem, may my right hand fail." Jahveh's faithful servants did not by any means withdraw from political affairs as if these were unclean or concerned the authorities only, or were things with which subjects had nothing to do. They felt most deeply the fate of their nation and took part with all their might in public affairs in the name of their God. The prophets in particular endeavoured with passionate ardour to guide the affairs of the State towards their own goal. We to-day cannot imitate these endeavours in detail,

WHAT IS LEFT OF THE OLD TESTAMENT? 43

but we may learn from them the lesson that an interest in politics and patriotism, on the one hand, and piety on the other, still belong together.

Further, it was on the basis of this national religion of Israel that the great idea of *Jahveh's sovereignty in history* arose. Again and again we read in the Old Testament that a comprehensive purpose of God runs through the entire history of Israel. That thought never loses its meaning, although it not rarely employs imperfect means and works with unhistorical or legendary materials. To express it in abstract terms, Revelation takes place in history. And the Old Testament even reached the thought that the heathen world also is included in God's purpose. In a famous chapter of Daniel (chapter vii.) the whole course of world history is summed up into a unity—four world kingdoms are to succeed each other on the stage. Here we have the conception of *world history*, and it is no mere accident that, almost down to the present day, our great historians have divided the history of the world in accordance with the four empires of Daniel. It is from Daniel that the modern world has learned the idea of a world history.

There have been other nations besides the Hebrews who possessed the gift of reflection on religious subjects. They have given forth difficult and complicated doctrines concerning what goes on within the Godhead or concerning the salvation of men. For example, there is the dogma of the Greek Christian Church, and there is the Scholasticism of the Middle Ages. We find nothing but faint hints of all that in the Old Testament. The Hebrew religion never got the length of actual dogmas. It was content with the statement of a few great principles. Compared with the truths set forth in the Old Testament, how difficult are even the Epistles of the New Testament, where the subtlety and acuteness of Hellenic thought are manifest! That is why it is so difficult to introduce our young people to-day to the thought of these Epistles. We are not concerned to deny that this is a weakness of the Hebrew mind. As long as it remained pure and untouched by outside influence, the Hebrew mind was hardly capable of philosophic thought. But to see this sheer simplicity is good for us, a generation whose spiritual world has come to be as complex as our social conditions.

Combined with this simplicity of the Hebrew mentality there is a *magnificent religious emotion*. By nature the Hebrew is more temperamental than a cold Northerner. No Greek ideal of moderation curbs his mind and heart. Unlike Christianity, his religion does not exhort him to gentleness, and his hot blood impels him to deeds of passionate energy, sometimes even of violence and fanaticism.

And as was the people, so was its history. This history is full of tragedies, nay, it is itself a great tragedy. The Greek people fights against the Persians, conquers them, and then enjoys its period of greatest glory; but the Hebrew people, once the equal of the Greeks in nobility and power of spirit, is again and again mercilessly crushed by the colossal world Powers.

Therefore it is not surprising that the Old Testament is a passionate book, full of hot blood, rich in great events and in mighty men. Nietzsche says: "In the Old Testament of the Jews, the book of Divine righteousness, there are men, events and words so great that there is nothing in Greek or Indian literature to compare with it."[1] And again: "We stand in awe in the

[1] *Beyond Good and Evil.*

WHAT IS LEFT OF THE OLD TESTAMENT? 45

presence of these tremendous reminders of what men used to be, and cannot fail to have our sad thoughts about ancient Asia and its peninsula Europe, which pretends, as compared with Asia, to stand for 'human progress.'" And Haller says:[1] "In that history there laughs and sobs, rejoices and wails, prays and rebels a soul, the soul of all those men who took part in the writing of this book: there fights and suffers and dies a people with a fate so tragic that the history of the world has never seen its equal."

The God of Israel, Who revealed Himself to Moses at Sinai, was originally a volcanic Deity. It was in the grandest but most awesome thing that earth has to show, viz. in a volcanic eruption, that Moses found his God. The thunders crash like the blare of trumpets. A heavy, dark cloud, pierced by the thunderbolts, covers the mountain. The whole mountain quakes. Flames shoot forth from the midst of the heavens. Or, moving with incredible speed, the smoke cloud rises, changing into ever new forms, lit up by the internal glow of the mountain. That is the "pillar of fire and smoke," "the glory of Jahveh," in which Jahveh reveals Himself. Jahveh was originally a volcanic God, and this characteristic of *suddenness* and *unexpectedness* He always retained. He may for long control Himself—the volcano does not erupt every day—but suddenly He rises to His sublime greatness and destroys in *one* fell blow all His enemies round about.

It is in keeping with this idea of the Deity that *War* was conceived by the people to be a special revelation of God; and with what terrible realism was Jahveh pictured as the God of War! Gentler natures may be filled with dismay at the thought of such a God,

[1] *Jahveh, Baal und Wir*, p. 11.

bespattered with blood; stronger natures will recognize in this conception the revelation of a mighty, gigantic power.

Dreadful were the deeds done for this dread God. Ancient Israel sacrificed to its God in the wild fury of war entire cities with all their inhabitants as an awful whole-offering. Elijah with his own hand cut down the prophets of Baal on the brook Kishon. At the word of Elisha, Jehu swept Baal out of Israel in a sea of blood. But these are only the excesses of the power of the faith that produced in Israel the grandest figures and ultimately led moral religion to victory through so many difficulties and storms.

It is in the Old Testament that we find the two greatest figures in Hebrew story. The first is Moses, such as Michelangelo—a kindred spirit—has figured him. High up on Mount Sinai he sits, holding in his hands the tables of the law, which he has received from God. From the valley at the foot of the mountain he hears a distant noise—it is a sound of war in the camp! No! It is no shout of victory, nor shout of vanquished men. He hears notes of melody. The people have fallen away from Jahveh and have cast a golden calf and are now celebrating a festival in its honour. Then the anger of Moses flares up; he hurls the tables, inscribed as they are by God's own hand, from him and smashes them to pieces on the ground. The saga which relates this deed imputes no blame to Moses in his fury. It understands full well that the extreme of passion befits the extreme of delinquency, and that a rage so fierce cannot but destroy.

The second great figure is Elijah on the same mountain. He is in the evening of his days. Throughout his long life he has wrestled for the soul of his people and failed

WHAT IS LEFT OF THE OLD TESTAMENT ? 47

to win it. All have fallen away, except "seven thousand men who have not bowed the knee to Baal." Wearied out, the prophet flees to the distant hill of God in order to lay his plaint before Jahveh Himself. And Jahveh appears to him and speaks consoling words. The dread judgment, so Jahveh tells him, is at hand. Three bloody "swords of Jahveh" are to cut down the faithless Israelites. These swords are the cruel king of their national enemy Aram, who will not even spare the child in the womb; the King of Israel itself, the savage Jehu, who will root out the royal dynasty and all other followers of Baal; and finally Elisha the prophet, Elijah's successor, who will slay "by the words of his mouth." In this manner will Israel be swept away and only the faithful seven thousand be left alive. What of that? In all that horror of blood it is Jahveh's judgment that is being accomplished. Jahveh's cause triumphs, and that is all that matters.

Moses and Elijah are succeeded by the writing prophets—Amos, Hosea, Isaiah, Jeremiah, Ezekiel—a great series of heroic figures, all "intoxicated with God," and upheld by the sublime thought that evil must have no place on earth, that a nation like Israel, so given over to sin, so faithless towards God, cannot continue to exist. Unlike the great men of former days, they do not appeal to the sword. Their sole weapon is the Word: in the interval the times have become softer. But in true greatness these representatives of God are not inferior to the ancients.

Let us take an example. The man of God[1] rises and stands, as it were, between heaven and earth. God has a controversy with His people. The prophet is God's spokesman. The judges are the hills around.

[1] Micah vi. 1-8.

> Hear 'the word' that Jahveh speaks!
> Up, plead 'before' the mountains
>   That the hills may hear thy voice.
> Listen, ye mountains, to the charge of Jahveh,
> 'Take note' ye strong places of the earth!
> For Jahveh has a charge against His people
>   And with Israel He enters into judgment.

This exordium is followed by the charge of Jahveh Himself—not, as we might expect, in anger and wrath, but in love and with gentle reproach:

> My people, what have I done to thee?
> And how have I crossed thee? Answer!
>   I brought thee out of Egypt
>   And delivered thee from the house of bondage.
> I called before thee Moses,
> Aaron, and Miriam 'with thee'[1]
> Remember what Balak ' ' suggested
> And what Balaam ' ' replied.

Balak, King of Moab, desired Balaam to curse Israel, but Balaam, under constraint by Jahveh, opened his mouth in blessing:

> From Sittim and Gilgal
> 'I made known my faithfulness for thy sake.'[2]

The words refer to the marvellous passage of Israel through the Jordan.

And now we are to suppose that Israel's heart is broken by those pleading words of love. Israel draws near to God in penitence, asking how it may atone for its sins:

> Wherewith shall I come before Jahveh,
> And bow down before the great God?
> Shall I come before Him with whole-offering
>   with calves a year old?
> Has He ' ' pleasure in thousands of rams,
> In ten thousands of rivers of oil?

---

[1] 'immecha.   [2] lema'anecha hōda'ti sidgathi.

The sacrifices thus offered are increasingly great, till ultimately they cannot be measured, but the last is the greatest:

> Shall I give my first born for my sin,
> The fruit of my body to atone for my soul?

The penitent sinner thus outbids himself, offering ever greater sacrifices, and finally reaches the most awful of all. But now it is as when the sun rises. Nothing of all that.

> 'It is told thee,' O man, what is good
> And what Jahveh desires at thy hand!
> Only this—do good, love mercy,
> And walk humbly before thy God.

An example like this shows better than many words the greatness of prophecy, the power of moral passion that dwelt in the prophets. Here we see how gloriously the power of the Old Testament religion can work.

The grandeur of this conception of God is shown with special clearness in the sublime conception of Creation. In other religions the deity may enter into the world, wrestle with its powers and finally reduce them to order. Jahveh is too great for that! He stands outside of the world and works from without upon it by His will. "God said: 'let there be light' and there was light." "In the beginning God created the heavens and the earth."

It is in keeping also with the greatness of this thought of God that Hebrew religion disdained every image of the Deity. It was not intelligent reflection, it was not illumination, it was profound fear of God that forbade every image, almost every symbol. To make an image is to make a comparison, but "'Where is the image with which ye can compare Me?' saith the Holy One."

It is this profound feeling of the greatness of God that explains the great part played by the *hymn* in practical religion. Of course, in the Hebrew religion there is present the universal human motive, according to which the pious man seeks from God the deliverance of his nation, his own salvation, and the fulfilment of earthly desires—a thought which undeniably appears repeatedly in the New Testament with many marks of human limitation. But side by side with it we find in great strength the nobler idea that man must have something besides himself, beyond himself, that he can look up to and worship, and to which he can devote himself with his whole soul. This deep need was profoundly felt by the men of the Old Testament—hence the richness and variety of the moving hymns in which God's praise is sung.

In addition to the warmth of these songs of praise, we find in the Old Testament expression of the *fear* of the Holy God. Hebrew religion is essentially a holy religion. "Woe is me, for I am undone, for I am a man of unclean lips, for mine eyes have seen the King, Jahveh Zebaoth." We could desire for our own people and their religion something of this depth of feeling that is so manifest in the Hebrew people and in their religion. The Old Testament, in its rugged strength, would be as iron in the blood for our time, which has become so soft, so irresolute, and so "out of joint."

To be sure, not everything in the Old Testament bears in equal degree this mark of sternness. The softer and tenderer notes of religion also find expression in it. Even genial and cheerful features are found, especially in the later writings. There are numerous touching narratives and arresting psalms. But there is common to all these one feature which our generation sorely needs, and for which the profoundest minds of our day are hungering, viz. *certainty in religion.* To the men of whom we have been speaking religion was something quite different from a " view of the world," although the two are not completely disjoined. To them God is not an " auxiliary conception," nor a pale abstraction, but a real figure, close to their heart. They walk " before Him," they live with Him, as we commune with a friend whom we saw yesterday and will see again to-morrow, who is thinking of us, although we do not see him at the moment. But this must not be misunderstood. The Living God is to-day just as close to the heart as He was yesterday and as He will be to-morrow. Through this nearness of God and this certainty of faith the religious life gained in depth and warmth, and the religious personality received an inward strength which seems to us, with our weaker faith, like a distant goal far above us. Therefore we look up full of reverence and longing to the prophets, to whom it was vouchsafed to feel the reality of God. This is why the religious heart of all the ages has loved the Psalms so much and responded more readily to their appeal than to that of those earlier heroic figures, great but over-vehement. It is in this spiritual lyric poetry of the Psalms that the natural notes of piety are heard :

> Like the hart that pants
>   After streams of water,
> So panteth my soul,
>   ' Jahveh,' for Thee.
> ' What have I then ' in heaven ?
> Besides Thee I ask for nought on earth.
> My flesh and my soul may perish, ' '
> Jahveh is my portion for ever.

These are the basic words of religion in which generations still unborn will express their deepest feelings. The religion of the Psalms lives amongst us still; in our hearts it is more effective than many of the Christian dogmas. How many pious hearts there are whose real religion is contained in the words: "The Lord is my shepherd: I shall not want"! Let us also keep in mind the simple exhortation of the pious Tobias: "All thy days have God before thine eyes and in thine heart, and beware lest thou consentest to any sin or doest aught against the law of God." Would it not be a crime to keep these treasures of religion from our children?

There is one more feature of the Old Testament to which reference must be made. The Old Testament presents a *rich and varied gallery of personalities*. We have already mentioned many of them in this brief outline—prophets, singers, thinkers, heroes, poets, utterers of proverbs. But how many more there are! This wealth of religious personality is the real greatness of the Hebrew religion. For this reason alone it is an insult to the historical spirit even to name Babylonians and Egyptians in one breath with Israel. These civilizations are great because of things achieved by great masses of men under the domination of despots and priests: gigantic world empires, great walls and canals, huge structures. But these civilizations, especially that of Babylon, are entirely destitute of personal life. With regard to Egypt, an exception must be made in the Tell-el-Amarna period, when that country was affected by Semitic influence. Israel, on the other hand, was poor in technical achievement; apart from its temporary greatness under David, the State had little importance. The nation was never great in works of external civilization; but in the sphere of spiritual things it produced

WHAT IS LEFT OF THE OLD TESTAMENT?

the highest that was achieved anywhere throughout the East—human personality living its own life in the presence of God. *That* is the achievement of Hebrew prophecy. And because of that achievement, Israel is " the chosen people " and " salvation is of the Jews." There can be no dispute about the matter. Our own day, with its marvellous technical achievements and its comprehensive organization of labour, may bear comparison with the civilizations of Egypt and Babylon, but the complaint is heard more and more loudly that the personalities which the idealistic age produced so abundantly are beginning to die out, and that it is becoming more and more difficult for independent men to maintain their ground in face of the mighty machine that reduces everyone to the same pattern. Would not a dash of the spirit of ancient Israel be good for our spiritual life to-day ? If the prophets would but awake !

And now one word to gather together all the various points which have been raised in the foregoing pages. We have shown that it is only when we have made up our minds to surrender unreservedly the ancient doctrine of Inspiration that the Old Testament reveals its true greatness. We have brought it down from heaven to earth, and now it rises majestically before our eyes from earth to heaven. We have also seen that it contains much that appears to us far from admirable, many things that would be dangerous and destructive to our religion and morality, if they were carried over unintelligently into our time ; and scientific honour demands that we do not, like a bad advocate, lay emphasis only on the one side, but that, like a just judge, we frankly set forth both sides.

How, then, are we to read the Old Testament? There are two methods in which a book like this may be read.

The layman seeks out those passages which are intelligible to him and commend themselves to him, and leaves the rest aside. He is quite within his right in so doing. Teachers—if I may be permitted with all diffidence to touch upon the work of those who are experts in their own line—will, in the lower stages, proceed in the same fashion. The Old Testament must therefore be examined to find out what is useful in it for the Christian child of the present day. Many of the things which are still taught should be omitted. Of the "ceremonial law" only a few samples are needed; of the "tabernacle" and its vessels very little need be said. In the narrative portions much may be altogether passed over, and here much can be learned from modern criticism of the sources. For very young children the Old Testament must be explained in a Christian spirit. At this stage the right of interpretation, which has been used by all generations of Christianity, can be used with a good conscience, if with careful reserve. From this stage there should be gradual progress to the higher and the highest stages. The teacher should pass slowly and carefully to a more historical conception. It can, of course, never be the task of religious instruction to educate the spirit of historical criticism in school-children; but, at a time when the need of criticism has been awakened in the youthful mind in other spheres, the teacher must carefully allow it its place in this sphere also, in order that the adult, when he is later shown the Old Testament in a more historical view, may not cast it aside with distaste. To such pupils the teacher should present the Creation Story as a sublime poem full of lofty thoughts, and when dealing with the history of Elijah he should not forget to show that Jesus Himself drew a distinction between His spirit and that of Elijah. At

WHAT IS LEFT OF THE OLD TESTAMENT? 55

the highest stage, i.e. in the higher classes of the secondary school, the history of Israel should be taught scientifically, like modern or Greek history. The recoil of educated people from religion would certainly not be so great as it is at present if the higher schools had long ago met this necessary demand. The present writer knows quite well how slight these hints are and how great is the task he is laying on teachers. But the task is not an impossible one ; it can be successfully accomplished by a teacher who has in his own heart a reverent love for the Bible and for his pupils. Later in life the pupils will remember with gratitude and reverence both their teacher and the religious lessons they learned from his lips.

But in addition to the teaching of the Bible in schools there should be more teaching on the part of the clergy than has been the case up till now. In their teaching of young communicants, in their confirmation classes, and in their preaching they should aim at a clear presentation of the special meaning of the Old Testament and also of its defects. Here, again, one cannot fail to see the peculiar difficulties that arise from the fact that the preacher has before him people of different degrees of education. But here also the aim should be to inculcate an understanding love for the Old Testament.

Finally, there is the complete picture as the historian sees it. The mind that has undergone historical training sees not only beautiful incidents—he sees the History. To him it is clear that in every human effort and attainment there is and must be both " great " and " small," the sublime beside the ordinary. The inferior element does not repel the historian ; indeed, he loves history because, as a faithful picture of human nature, it contains, and must contain, these features. We see in it lofty thought and worthy life; but we see them not only as consolidated achievements, but also in the process of becoming, wrestling with lower elements and slowly freeing itself from these. It was only at the end of its history that Israel fully attained to the Monotheism towards which it was steering from the very beginning, and in many utterances, especially the poetical ones, we find it still entangled with remnants of polytheism. To a student with an historical turn of mind such a picture of struggling growth seems more attractive than that of a finished achievement. Even Christian faith will not be offended by this thought. The Old Testament is not the perfect revelation of the Christian view: it is only the revelation taking place in history.

The course taken by world history has made the spiritual life of Israel one of the foundations of the civilization of the Christian nations of Europe. Our civilization rests on two bases—the Bible, i.e. Old and New Testaments, and the civilization of Greece. We have become what we are in virtue of the combination of these two worlds. It would be a revolution, which no one living can estimate, if either of these foundations were to be moved. A man with an historical mind will consider it his duty to understand the Mind which is revealed in all history and which has set as a foundation these two pillars, and he will reach the conviction that, while the process of building goes on, its foundation-stones will abide.

II

FUNDAMENTAL PROBLEMS OF HEBREW LITERARY HISTORY[1]

THE aim of this essay is to give a short account of the main principles underlying my article on Hebrew Literature which appeared in *Kultur der Gegenwart*.[2]

Down to the present time there is, properly speaking, nothing that can be called a history of Hebrew literature, although much valuable preliminary work has been done. There is, of course, a branch of study, usually called Old Testament Introduction, which deals mainly with the critical questions that concern the literature. For many years these critical problems have occupied the most prominent place in Old Testament study. That was just and right, and criticism will always remain an important, even a fundamental, branch of Old Testament scholarship. Some of the Old Testament writings have come down to us without any statement regarding the date when they were composed. In the case of others, traditional statements on that subject have been proved to be erroneous. We have learned that many of the books in the Old Testament have a very complicated history. They have been compiled from older oral or written traditions and have been subjected to frequent redaction. It was the first duty of scholarship to clear this jungle before undertaking any constructive

[1] First published in *Deutsche Literaturzeitung*, Jahrgang xxvii, 1906, columns 1797–1800, 1861–1866. Reprinted in my *Reden und Aufsätze*, p. 29 ff.   [2] Vol. i, 1906, pp. 51–102.

work. Even if some of the results reached can only be called tentative, this task has now been practically accomplished, and it is now possible to build on this foundation and make an attempt towards constructing the history of Hebrew literature.

Many scholars will at once raise the objection that no such history can be given. To begin with, the chronology of the writings is quite uncertain. In many cases the most that can be done is to assign the writing in question to a period. To arrange all the books and their constituent parts in anything like a fixed chronological order is quite impossible. Again, we have no knowledge of the writers. In many cases we do not even know their names, and there is hardly a single case where we have reliable information regarding the personal circumstances and career of the writer. From this it is clear that a history of Hebrew literature, meaning an indication of the chronological order of the Old Testament writings and an exposition of each writing in the light of the personality of the author of it, cannot possibly be written.

But now the question arises whether, notwithstanding this, there cannot be a history of Hebrew literature in a different sense. The lack of a definite chronology would not be an insuperable obstacle. We should have to be content with indicating the periods of literary activity and dispense with more definite statements. In the case of such ancient literature the personalities of the writers are of far less importance than in the literature of later ages. In the great periods of later literatures, literary history must necessarily take the form of biographies of the great writers and their works must be interpreted through their personal experiences. But in ancient Israel personality, even in the case of an author, was far less developed. In the Psalms, for instance, we find an extraordinary sameness of content—in different Psalms we find the same thoughts, moods, forms of expression, metaphors, rhetorical figures, phrases. Even the very greatest writers in Israel, the prophets, frequently exhibit the most striking uniformity. This is due to the fact that in antiquity the power of custom was far greater than it is in the modern world, and besides, like everything else connected with religion, religious literature—and the writings contained in the Old Testament are almost exclusively religious—is very conservative. Therefore a history of Hebrew literature, if it is to do justice to its subject-matter, has comparatively little concern with the personality of the writers. That has, of course, a place of its own, but Hebrew literary history should occupy itself more with the literary type that lies deeper than any individual effort. Hebrew literary history is therefore the history of the literary types practised in Israel, and it is perfectly possible to produce such a history from the sources that are available.

The prime task of a history of literature in Israel must therefore be to determine the *literary types* represented in the Old Testament. We must take the writings of the Old Testament, and, as many of these are collections of writings, we must take their constituent parts out of the order in which they happen to appear in our Canon and in which " Old Testament Introduction " usually studies them, and then rearrange them according to the type to which they belong.

Some of the main literary types may be briefly mentioned. There is first the broad classification into Prose and Poetry. Narrative is usually found in prose form, and the following different kinds of narrative can be distinguished : stories about the deities, i.e. Myths ; primitive Folk-tales (of these two, only fragments are found in Israel); the popular Saga; the longer Romance; the religious Legend; and, lastly, Historical Narrative in the stricter sense. Poetical literary types include: the oracular wisdom, the prophetic oracular saying, the Lyric—the two last mentioned being specially frequent. Lyric poetry is again subdivided into (*a*) secular lyrics, such as the Dirge, the Love Song, the scornful lay, the song of carouse, the wedding song, the song of victory, the royal song, and (*b*) spiritual lyrics, including the Hymn, the Thanksgiving, the Dirge (both private and public, the Eschatological Psalm, etc. Numerous types are found conjoined in the prophetic writings—the Vision in narrative form, the Prophetic Oracle, the Discourse (in many forms). Among these last mentioned the oldest is that which foretells the future, and may either be the Threat or the Promise; the Invective, upbraiding sin; the Exhortation, calling to well-doing, and many others. Most of these types have long been recognized, and it is the task of Literary History to study them systematically and scientifically. Each type must be studied in order to show the materials with which it deals and the forms which it necessarily assumes. It will be found that a particular literary type is distinguished by a certain form of exordium. Just as the fairy-tale of to-day usually opens with " Once upon a time," a letter with " Dear Sir," a sermon with " Brethren," so the Hebrew Hymn frequently opens with " Sing unto the Lord," the Dirge with " Ah! How," the Prophetic Invective with " Ha! Ye." It is possible that students who are still unfamiliar with these ancient types will at first find it difficult to recognize them, definite and distinct as they are, but we must remember that this difficulty did not exist for the ancient world. To the people of Israel the laws of literary form were as familiar as the rules of Hebrew grammar. They obeyed them unconsciously and lived in them; it is only we who have to learn to understand them. Professor Karl Budde was the first to describe one ancient Hebrew literary type, the Dirge. It was he also who made out the Wedding Song and thus encouraged others to undertake similar studies. In more recent days, Hedwig Tahnor has described the Hebrew Dirge in all its varieties and compared it with similar poems of primitive peoples.

It goes without saying that a task of this kind calls for an artistic sense which up till now has not been very prominent in Old Testament " Introduction." But this æsthetic sense must not be content to express delight over the beauty of ancient Hebrew compositions. It must endeavour to dissect understandingly the beauty that is there, and scholars will then perhaps abandon the view that the æsthetic treatment of the Old Testament writings is unscientific and should be left to " popular " writers.

This study of the literary types, however, will only merit the name of Literary History when it attempts to get at the *history through which these types have passed*.

Every ancient literary type originally belonged to a quite definite side of the national life of Israel. Just as among ourselves the " sermon " belongs to the pulpit, while the " fairy-tale " has its home in the nursery, so in ancient Israel the Song of Victory was sung by maidens to greet the returning war-host; the Lament was chanted by hired female mourners by the bier of the dead; the Thora was announced by the priest in the sanctuary; the Judgment (*mishpat*) was given by the judge in his seat; the prophet uttered his Oracle in the outer court of the temple; the elders at the gate gave forth the Oracle of Wisdom. To understand the literary type we must in each case have the whole situation clearly before us and ask ourselves, Who is speaking? Who are the listeners? What is the *mise en scène* at the time? What effect is aimed at? In many cases a type is employed by a special class of speaker, and its use reveals of what class he is. Just as to-day a " sermon " implies a professional " preacher," so in ancient times the Thora and the hymn of worship were given through the priest, the oracular saying was uttered by the " wise men," and the lay was the utterance of a " singer." There may even have been a professional class of popular " story-tellers."

Only a short study of these literary types is needed to show that, almost without exception, they were originally not written, but spoken. It is another of the profound differences between ancient Hebrew life and the life of modern days that writing dominated life and even " literature " to a far less extent than it does with us. This explains the extreme brevity and small compass of the ancient compositions. This deserves to be strongly emphasized, because modern students, accustomed to much longer compositions, find it difficult to understand such brevity, and because the delimitation of the literary units is an essential postulate of any literary history. It is a familiar fact that a hearer is able to grasp much longer literary units than a reader, who can, of course, suspend and resume his reading at will. This is especially true of the ancient listener, whose receptive power was very limited. Therefore the units of ancient times, both spoken and sung, are much shorter than the written ones with which we are more familiar to-day. The most ancient Hebrew national ballad is contained in one or perhaps two long lines—

PROBLEMS OF HEBREW LITERARY HISTORY 63

that was all the average hearer of the day could grasp at a time. The Wisdom literature existed originally as single proverbs or sayings, only one being put forth at a time. And even the most ancient legal judgments, prophetic utterances, and Thora statutes are not much longer. In the Sagas we can make out an ancient style in which the narrative originally consisted of not more than two or three of our modern Bible " verses."

It is still possible, in the case of many of these literary types, to trace how they gradually became longer. Compare, for instance, the lengthy utterances of Ezekiel with those " burdens," mostly quite brief, of which the " Book " of Amos is composed ; or the detailed Joseph Romance with the brief Saga of the Tower of Babel. Just as we see the development of our children's minds in the gradually increasing amount that they can take in at a time, so we can trace one feature of the growth of civilization in the gradual increase of the literary units in Israel. Finally, it is true in contrast to the ancient brevity of style, an entirely new tendency arose, a tendency that resulted in tediousness, such as we find in the long-drawn-out speeches in Deuteronomy, in some passages of Jeremiah, in the already-mentioned Joseph Romance, in a Psalm like the cxixth. Without doubt this drift towards length indicates that the times had grown more literary.

But it is one of the critical moments in the life of an ancient literature when some of the types that originally belonged to the life of the people appear in definitive written form. Then, as a rule, *collections of writings* appear. Almost all that we have in the " Books " of the Old Testament comes under this category. It is among the people that the single proverb, the single song, the single narrative emerges ; but when these are reduced to writing, naturally several of them are put together. Thus arise collections of Sagas, Lays, and Proverbs. Such collections are of various kinds. Sometimes the original brief units are simply put together without any connection between the items, as in the case of our hymn-books, or Grimm's Tales, the Old Testament Psalter, the book of Proverbs, and in many of the prophetic books. In that case the chief literary interest lies not so much in the " Books," as in the shorter units which were afterwards gathered into " Books." In other cases, the compilers have conjoined shorter units to form longer units, and these together constitute a new separate entity, i.e. a " Book." Thus most of the so-called Historical Books of the Old Testament are made up of oral traditions, which have been woven —sometimes by a complicated process—into some degree of unity by professional writers and infused with their spirit. Here, again, Literary History is specially interested in these collectors, who did more than merely collect the material. Then, lastly, there emerged great creative personalities, who followed up the artificial work of less gifted men and produced new, more comprehensive units. Thus, in the days when the author of Job lived, there must have been an abundant literature of Songs and Sayings; but that genius proceeded to create complete cycles of long speeches and worked them up into one splendid comprehensive poem.

There is another line of the history of these literary types which runs parallel with that which has been described above. The ancient types grew up among the people and were part of their national genius. By and by arose professional writers—Poets, Story-tellers, Prophets—who employed the styles that had been perfected by the people and applied them for their own purposes. Thus artistic poetry arose out of the national poetry. Less gifted men adopted a style as they found it; abler men added here and there something of their own; men of genius transformed it. Each type had its classical period. Then came the mere imitators. In many parts of the Old Testament we have side by side examples of the oldest popular composition, classical creations, and fainter imitations—of the last named more than a few. Our science has the task of describing the mentality and the work of these writers, and the exposition of the great writers of Israel is the copestone of the Hebrew Literary History. It will be clear from what has been said that a true appreciation of these men is only possible when the types have been studied. We must also keep in view that a writer who employs a type which he has borrowed may use it in various ways. There is no foundation for the fear that such a study of the types will push into the background the more important study of the writers. The two lines of study in no way exclude each other, but scholars should meantime devote attention first to what is really the primary task—the study of the types.

The oldest types, in the form in which they were current among the people, are always *pure* and unmixed; but in later periods, when men and conditions of life were more complex, when professional writers adopted the type, there occur deviations and mixtures of styles. The Dirge, e.g., which was originally sung at the grave of a dead man, was used metaphorically in connection with the downfall of a people or of a city. At a still later stage it was employed to express scornful exultation over a fallen enemy. Again, religious songs, originally used in divine service, were sometimes divorced from such public use and were sung by an individual in his own chamber. It was in this way that the Psalm poetry arose. Or, again, we find a combination of song and proverb or song conjoined with narrative. All manner of mixed styles are specially frequent in the prophets. In their eagerness to reach their people they adopted a very large number of types used by other writers, combined them, and filled them with prophetic content. It was thus the prophets became poets, historians, and legislators, and the types which they thus used and developed were continued by their disciples as independent types. Such mingling of styles is frequently found when the history of a literature is nearing its close.

Occasionally it is even possible to see the same material passing through different literary types, being transformed on each occasion in the spirit of a new age. For instance, the Saga can be seen passing into the Romance and into the Legend.

Finally we come to the tragedy of Hebrew literature. The spirit loses power. The types are exhausted. Imitations begin to abound. Redactions take the place of original creations. Hebrew ceases to be the living language of the people. By this time the collections are grouped together into larger collections. The Canon has come into being.

It need hardly be said that the Literary History of Israel, having such tasks to perform, must perforce take the shape of historical narrative. Old Testament Introduction may consider it sufficient to treat its problems separately, following the accidental order in which the books have come down to us. Some attempts have been made, even from that standpoint, to produce something to which the name of Literary History has been given. But a genuine History of the literature can only be founded on a thorough study of the types. Its character must be determined by a consideration of the types and of the periods into which the history of the nation and its civilization falls. It will only merit the title it claims when it can show how the literature emerged from the national history and was the expression of its spiritual life. Professor Reuss, in his *Geschichte der Reiligen Schriften des Alten Testaments*, has done much to prepare the way for a real Literary History of Israel.

There remains one more point of great importance. The history of Israel has very close connections with the history of the other Oriental peoples, and therefore, in the study of its literature, constant attention must be paid to the cognate literary types that were current among these peoples, especially in Babylonia and Egypt. In this regard Old Testament scholars have still a large debt to pay. The time is now surely past when men will try to interpret the oracles of the Old Testament without regard to the similar literature of Egypt, or to understand the religious songs of Israel apart from those of Babylonia. This study is still in its infancy, and a rich harvest awaits the student who endeavours to collect all the narratives, including those of distant nations, that exhibit any likeness to those of Israel and compare them with each other. Very curious affinities will be recognized, but on the other hand the peculiar character of the Hebrew mind will be all the more clearly seen. Such a task is, to be sure, far beyond the power of any one man. Can we not have an Academy, a brotherhood of scholars, who feel the importance of the subject and are willing to follow it up?

Although Literary History presupposes the settlement of the main problems of "Introduction," it will doubtless also have a reflex influence on that branch of study. It will save scholars from giving exclusive interest to mere details and direct their minds to larger problems. It will also shed new light on many aspects of Hebrew life. When we have seen how literary types arise, and understand that they are not the creations of individual men, but are produced by the co-operation of many generations, we shall not be likely to claim that one man—say Jeremiah—wrote the Psalms of Israel. Further, the influence of oral tradition on the literature will be seen to be greater than has yet been admitted.

The author's article on the "Literaturgeschichte Israels" in *Kultur der Gegenwart* attempts in fifty pages to indicate what can be done in this direction. In view of the wide reach of the task, he is unable to say when he will be in a position to add anything to what he has there said.[1]

[1] Cf. the article "Bibelwissenschaft IC: Literaturgeschichte, Israels" in *Religion in Geschichte und Gegenwart*, and the numerous other literary articles there.

III

THE RELIGION OF THE PSALMS [1]

DISCUSSION about the value of the Old Testament for the Protestant Church has not yet come to an end in Germany. The best interests of our Church, however, demand that this discussion should be carried on not with an excess of zeal for or against the Old Testament, but with calm impartiality and thorough knowledge of the subject, and therefore an Old Testament subject is specially relevant to our business here to-day.

We are to deal with a theme that lies at the very heart of the Old Testament, or at least constitutes one of its chief interests. In former days the Psalms were awarded a place almost equal to that occupied by the New Testament. To-day we are not to treat any of the external questions, although, of course, scholarship cannot evade them: we are to leave unmentioned all critical problems and all questions of date. We are to consider now exclusively the most characteristic content of the Psalter, the religion that finds expression there.

The material that is to occupy us now is extremely varied and complicated. It can also be fairly said that up till now this subject has been neglected. The task of the present day is to lay a foundation for the understanding of the Psalms. The purpose of this lecture is not to lay that foundation, but rather to put before you some results of that preliminary work. In order to

[1] A lecture delivered in the Bund für Gegenwartschristentum, Eisenach, October 4, 1921. First published in *Die Christliche Welt*, xxxvi, 1922, Nos. 1, 2, 5, 6, and 7.

make these results intelligible, I must say a very few words about the kind of foundation work to which I have referred.

If we are to reach a clear view of these poems, with all their numerous similarities and divergences, our first business must be to arrange them in groups according to their literary types. This does not mean, however, any capricious classification in accordance with individual taste. Our aim is to restore the arrangement that indicates the origin and source of the Psalms. This is, or should be, the prime interest of all study of the book at the present time, and should include a study of the rise and the history of Hebrew psalmody. I have already hinted at such a study in my *Reden und Aufsätze* and in the article " Psalmen " in Schiele-Zscharnack's Lexicon called *Religion in Geschichte und Gegenwart*, and I shall return to it at greater length in my *Einleitung zu den Psalmen*, which is about to be published. Here and now I shall enumerate a few of the chief results.

1. If we are to understand the Psalms as living poetry, we must not confine ourselves to the songs contained in the Psalter. We must include the cognate poetry in the historical books, in the book of Job, in the prophetical writings, in the Apocrypha, as well as the lyric poetry of other peoples, especially the Babylonians and the Egyptians. And we are discussing here to-day not only the piety of the Psalter, but that of Hebrew lyric poetry as a whole. We can, of course, on the present occasion give only a brief sketch of the subject.

2. Our most important task is to understand how this poetry arose. As in the case of all the literature of Israel, we must think of the Psalms as primarily not written literature at all. We must put away all thoughts

of paper and ink and look on the Psalms as having their source in the life of the people. They played a part there before they took literary form at all. The most important fact in this connection is that the singing of Psalms was originally a part of worship. In certain parts of worship, both public and private, songs were sung, and the most important aspect of the history of psalm-singing is that it spread beyond the public sanctuary and penetrated into the private worship of the pious individual. The individual imitated the models which were familiar to him in public worship and filled them with his own personal life.

3. We are thus able to classify the Psalms according to their types. These songs are to be arranged according to the aspect of religious life to which they originally belong. They are differentiated into:

Hymns, originally sung as choruses or solos at a sacred feast.

Songs of Praise, akin to the hymns used in public thanksgivings.

National Dirges, rendered by the choir at times of national stress or calamity.

Court Songs, sung by the Court singer in the temple in presence of the royal Court.

Individual Dirges, originally sung in the sanctuary by individuals in times of personal stress, such as sickness, whether in protestation of innocence or in acknowledgment of sin, and then used by such individuals at home to relieve their feelings.

Individual Songs of Praise, originally sung to accompany a thank-offering for deliverance out of great distress.

There are also minor or secondary types, which bear evidence of having been influenced by the prophetical writings and by the Wisdom literature, such as that represented by the Proverbs of Solomon.

Now if we wish to look at the inner life of the Psalmists we must start from these types, and we shall do well to take together the types that are most closely akin. We shall thus have a clear view of the aspects presented by the religious life of Israel, so far as that finds expression in religious lyric poetry. Such aspects comprise:

(1) *The Religion of the Hymns*, in which the fundamental thoughts and feelings find expression.
(2) *The Religion of the People*, contained in the National Dirges and Songs of Praise and Hymns, and in the eschatological poetry in imitation of the prophets.
(3) *The Religion of the Court*, found in the Court Psalms.
(4) *The Religion of the pious individual*, as revealed in Dirges and Songs of Praise and Lyric Wisdom Poetry.

1. THE HYMNS.

These were sung to the accompaniment of instruments by, or in the presence of, the assembled congregation at a sacred festival. Therefore, in order to appreciate poems of this kind, we must have as clearly as possible before our eyes a picture of such a celebration. From far and near the people have gathered together at the sanctuary. They are all there in gladsome mood. The grace of Jahveh has blessed the land and there is once more abundance of bread. Almost all the great regular festivals of ancient Israel were harvest festivals. On these occasions the sanctuary, the priests, and all the worshippers appeared in their best array. It was a time of great rejoicing and of eating and drinking. Chiefest of all were the varied solemn services in which the individual could take part—including the feastings. Evidently an important place was given to large dance processions in which the whole assemblage joyously took share. These festivities were the red-letter days of Israel from the earliest down to the latest times. In the earlier days they did much to promote the unification of the people, and at a later time they were the actual centre round which the Jewish community clustered. That community was able to cohere because it had these celebrations in Jerusalem, just as the varied peoples of Islam find their bond of unity to-day in the celebrations at Mecca. To take part in one of these feasts was the greatest ambition of the Jew living in the Dispersion. Even if at a later time he had to pine in misery and want, far from the sanctuary, beset by unbelieving enemies, he still remembered with longing those festive times in which he had been enabled to share :

> How once I went ' to the tent of the Glorious One '
>   to the house of Jahveh,
> amid the strains of joy and praise,
>   ' the revelry ' of the pilgrims.[1]   (Ps. xlii. 5.)

The Book of Ecclesiasticus shows clearly how deep was the impression made on the pilgrim by such a celebration, when the high priest came forth from the temple in all the splendour of his official robes and with his

[1] The single commas ' ' indicate emendations of the text. Defence of the translations will be found in my Commentary *Die Psalmer* 1926.

own hands laid the sacrifice on the altar, when the attendant priests blew their trumpets and the singers raised their voices in praise (Ecclus. l). At such a moment all present realized their unity as a people—a glorious thought for the Jew whose lot in life had led him to a far-off land. At such times he realized Jahveh's glory and presence. The technical expression for being present in the sanctuary was "to see Jahveh," "to behold the beauty of the Lord," i.e. to be conscious of His presence.

It is the spiritual content of such experiences that finds expression in the Hymns. The leading *motifs* of these poems are therefore zeal, devotion, awe, thanksgiving, and praise. Of course these are the characteristic notes of Hebrew religion at all times, but they are specially prominent in the Hymns. The same holds good, indeed, in other religions, especially those of Babylon and of Egypt, but it is a distinguishing feature of Hebrew religion and a token of its outstanding worth that these *motifs* should be so predominant. "Let my first thought be thanks and praise." In the Babylonian Hymns we frequently find petition added to praise; the deity is first flattered in order that he may be moved to grant the request. Such petition is hardly ever found in the Hebrew Hymn, and the Hymn thus represents the deepest and noblest religious need of man, to kneel in the dust and worship that which is higher than himself. It is no self-seeking piety that finds voice in the Hymns.

This explains the splendid objectivity which marks the view taken of human life in the hymns of Israel. When, e.g., the subject of the hymn is Jahveh's omnipotent rule among men, how He brings low the rich and humiliates the mighty, the poet's heart is filled, not

THE RELIGION OF THE PSALMS

with sadness at the thought of the transitoriness of all that is human, but with joy at the thought of God's greatness. The standpoint of the poet is not that of man who rises or falls, but that of God who can bring low or lift up as He wills. Hence, the hymn-singer does not shrink from describing the dread side of Jahveh's character. Take that mighty hymn of the thunderstorm, Psalm xxix. Even that is a theme for praise—the fact that He is so terrible!

This singing of praise to God has, of course, a great effect on the singer. Religious thought gathers strength when it is strongly expressed. The individual worshipper is borne along by the universal enthusiasm. Hence these hymns, in which the whole people can join with loud voice, can be deep experiences for individual worshippers; but this subjective, personal aspect finds little or no expression. *The Hymn is sung for God alone.*

The Hebrew Hymn has borne the fairest of blossoms. The Babylonian and Egyptian Hymns consist mainly of a lifeless enumeration of divine attributes. Even some of the hymns in the Bible are hackneyed and trite enough, but there are many majestic in power and throbbing with life. "The heavens declare the glory of God" (Ps. xix). "Holy is Jahveh of Hosts. All lands are full of His glory" (Is. vi. 3).

These hymns reveal very impressively how strong was the enthusiasm of the nation for its God. No language could adequately express the feelings of the people as they gathered together for His worship. Again and again we come upon the exhortation that not only the rejoicing Jews should thus sing praises to the Lord, but that all peoples, all creatures, all realms of nature must add their voices if His name is to be worthily magnified. The hymn of the seraphs in Is. vi. 3 was sung with such power that the pillars of the heavenly palace were shaken—*that* is how Jahveh should be praised ! To take part in such worship was the dearest duty and the highest privilege of the individual. The heavens are Jahveh's ; them He has reserved for Himself. But the earth He has given to the sons of men. The dead cannot praise Him ; in the silence of Sheol His praise is not heard. But we who live in this world and can sing—let us praise Him evermore (Ps. cxv. 16). The singing of praise to Jahveh is thus an essential part of religious service. Enthusiasm for God is an essential element in the religious life.

From all this it is clear that it is the objective side of religion that is most prominent in the Hymn—Jahveh Himself, His deeds and His attributes. That is why we are giving priority of place to this literary type. But we must also keep in view the outstanding importance attached to the awe and enthusiasm that are aroused in His presence.

What does the Hymn say about Jahveh ? Its constant themes are such as these. He is the Incomparable. Among the gods there is none like Him in holiness, power, wisdom, and goodness. His dwelling is in the heavens, and this very fact, that He has His throne in this loftiest part of the world, indicates that He Himself is the " Highest." The same idea is found in Babylonian and Egyptian hymns, but it is only among the Hebrews that His appearance is seen in the terrors of the lightning and in volcanic eruptions (Ps. xxix). This is an ancient conception that goes back to the revelation given at Sinai. But the Hymns contain various other mythological views of nature. The light is His garment ; the clouds are His chariots ; the winds and the lightnings

THE RELIGION OF THE PSALMS

are His servants. But side by side with this antique phraseology there is another, a supernatural manner of speech according to which the phenomena of nature are not only manifestations of God, but the works of His hands. " He commanded and it stood fast " (Ps. xxxiii. 9). In this connection it is, of course, mainly upon those striking phenomena which the ancients were unable to explain that attention is directed. Well-known examples are found in Job and in the famous Hymn of Creation, Ps. civ. Here we see also the *characteristic optimism* of Hebrew religion—the world is good, and God is its wise and gracious creator. Such Psalms are all the more precious in that they form a supplement to the New Testament, in which comparatively little is said about nature.

The Hymns also exalt *the doings of Jahveh in the past*. In Babylonian and Egyptian hymns dealing with this subject, mythological allusions are frequent, and similar material is not altogether absent from the Hebrew Hymn.

Rahab Thou didst crush	like carrion
with strong arm	Thou scatteredst Thy foes :
Thine are the heavens	Thine the earth ;
The world and what fills it	Thou hast founded.

(Ps. lxxxix. 11.)

In the previous verse we read :

| Thou abidest Lord | over the insolence of the sea |
| ' at the tumult ' of its waves | Thou stillest them. |

Here Rahab is the sea-monster whom Jahveh subdued before the creation and from whose power He delivered the world. There is another mythical echo in the majestic xixth Psalm, where the glory of the solar ball is likened to that of a youthful hero. And there are other similar allusions.

It is no mere chance that the Creation Myth should find such a prominent place in this Hymn type of poetry. The creation of the world by God is one of the chief themes of the Hymns even among other peoples, because in that work the omnipotence of God is especially revealed.

This supplies a clue to a part of the history of the religion of Israel. The Hebrew mind, *pari passu* with its development along its own lines, took up an attitude increasingly antagonistic to myth, and that element became fainter and fainter till it ultimately disappeared. Its place was taken by the *Sacred Legend*. We have a whole series of hymns which sing the praise of the God who led Israel in the days of old, and which borrow their material for this purpose from the narrative books which were by that time in existence and contained many traditional and legendary elements. Examples are Ps. cv. 14, Exod. xv. We see here how the great thought—proclaimed with such zest by the prophets—that the history of Israel was a fellowship between Jahveh and His people, edified and helped later generations. This adoption of the Legend into the Hymn is a phenomenon peculiar to Hebrew hymnody. There is nothing like it in the hymns of Babylon or Egypt. The recurrent theme of such legendary hymns is the story of the Passover—a proof of the deep impression made by that feast on the religious mind in Israel.

But the Hymns have also much to say about *Jahveh in the future*. He is the God who was and is, and is to come. The heart of the pious Hebrew thrills when he thinks of the time that is to come, when Jahveh will reveal Himself in His true majesty and ascend the

THE RELIGION OF THE PSALMS

throne of the world. This is another manifest proof how the preaching of the prophets influenced the hymns. The favourite method followed by the singer when thinking of this theme was to project himself into these latter days, with the result that to him the coming event was as if it had already happened. This impressive figure, exemplified in Pss. xlvi and cxlix, was borrowed by the hymn-singer from the prophets.

There is another way in which we can see how the prophets influenced the hymn-singers. Now and again the latter borrowed the finest thoughts of the prophets and embodied them in their hymns. In Ps. ciii. 11, 13, we read :

> As high as heaven is above the earth,
> So ' high ' is His grace over His worshippers ;
> As a father shows pity to his children,
> So Jahveh pitieth His worshippers.

Still another and quite a peculiar result of prophetic influence on the Hymns is found in the *prophetic Invective* that is occasionally added to a Hymn. While the people, assembled in the sanctuary, are joyously extolling the greatness of God, they hear in a voice of thunder, that recalls the prophetic style, the exhortation, " Now, repent ye yourselves " (Pss. lxxxi and xcv). In such Hymns we have an impressive presentation of the two aspects of the religion—joy in God and the grave demands that He makes.

It was only very rarely and not till a late period that enthusiasm for *the Law* found voice in the Hymns. One example is found in Ps. xix. 8-11. Sober, earnest study of the Law, and the enthusiasm that finds expression in the Hymn, belong essentially to different worlds.

One step of the evolution through which the Hymn

passed is one that can also be seen in other literary types, viz. it was extended from public worship into personal religion and private devotion. As a rule the Hymn was sung by the choir, but from the very beginning there was a Solo rendered by a skilled singer. Solo hymns of this kind were by and by sung by the individual at times when there was neither feast nor congregation, and a gifted singer could occasionally pour his personal religion into this mould. Ps. ciii presents a fine example of how a singer could pour forth his heartfelt gratitude for restoration from sickness in the Hymn form: "Bless the Lord, O my soul"; and in Ps. cxxxix we see how a singer can add to his Hymn many profound thoughts regarding the relation between God and His worshipper: "O God, Thou searchest me and knowest me."

To sum up: In his Hymn the pious man kneels in worship and adoration and proclaims with full heart to all the world the glory of God.

2. The Religion of the People.

Our first source for the popular religion is the National Dirge. When harvest had failed, or when pestilence had come, or an enemy was at the gate, the people assembled at the sanctuary, rent their garments, fasted, wept, and prayed. A trumpet was blown in order that the sound might reach to heaven. This was the national mourning service—an entire nation passionately beseeching their God to have mercy upon them.

Part of such a service was the singing of a Dirge. Between these Dirges and the Hymns there is the strongest possible contrast. That we should find together in the Psalter the Song of Praise with its

THE RELIGION OF THE PSALMS

enthusiasm and the Dirge with its note of woe shows the contrasts that exist in the religion of the Psalms. One thing is common to both—they have the same intensity of passion; passionate enthusiasm in the Hymn, passionate wailing and praying in the Dirge. This emotional intensity, indeed, is a distinctive quality of Israel, its religion, and its religious lyric poetry.

These Dirges are so many cries of despair wrung from a tortured nation—cries the like of which have perhaps never been heard anywhere else in this world. Let us look first at *what they contain*. The Dirges in the Psalter are almost all of a political nature. From the Assyrian period onwards, Israel, which had been hemmed in throughout its history by enemies, was fated to pass from one foreign oppression to another. Even in postexilic days the Jewish community of Jerusalem was only a small colony, annoyed and oppressed by malevolent neighbours, and as time went on that community suffered continued disruption, till it was dispersed over the whole East. Wherever he went the Jew was unpopular, the butt of scorn, whose life and property were alike unsafe. Besides, their internal conditions were wretched. We hear repeatedly in the Individual Dirges of the two opposing parties. The rich and the great were on the point of falling away both from their religion and their nationality, and showed a disposition to ally themselves with like-minded men among foreign peoples. They ruthlessly exploited the poor and the lowly. These distressful circumstances, on the surface political and social, were felt by religious minds to be also *moral* and *religious*. Men of this temper were horrified to see everywhere the same spectacle—lies and disloyalty triumphant, blood poured out like water, captives crying for liberty, the innocent for justice.

Conditions like these were all the more intolerable to men who had been taught by the prophets to love righteousness and justice. But they also constituted a religious problem. God, extolled in the Hymns as a refuge for the oppressed, seemed to be idly looking on while so much innocent blood was shed. When would He come to smite the oppressor and bring down the proud? God, who had chosen Israel, allowed the heathen to defile His inheritance, and merely listened while the foreigner taunted and mocked the puny, miserable nation. This scorn from the foreigner was very galling to the proud Jew and is frequently mentioned. Nor was this all. The heathen turned their mockery on Jahveh Himself and blasphemed His name, speaking contemptuously of the god whose people they had subjugated; and even Jews themselves were losing faith and turning away from Him, saying, " There is no God." Added to all this was the influence of the polytheism that prevailed in the whole world around them. There were even Jews who no longer dared to deny that the gods of the nations were real powers, even if they still ranked these deities far beneath Jahveh. Such deities must be vassals of Jahveh, to whom He had for a time entrusted dominion. But they had abused the power He had lent to them and thrown the world into confusion. Lord, Jahveh, take out of their hands the power that is Thine, and become Thyself the monarch of the world!

These Dirges are thus the cry of a nation that refused at all costs to bow to the fate that Providence had laid upon it, and felt anew each day the hurt done to its most sacred feelings. And religion gave the despair an even keener edge. Faith in Jahveh was flatly contradicted by experience. Hence the ever recurring,

THE RELIGION OF THE PSALMS 83

despairing note, " Why ? " that characterizes the Dirges. Why burns His wrath against the sheep of His pasture ? Why hast Thou forgotten the promises of former days ? Why didst Thou cause us to err from Thy ways ? There is no attempt and no inclination to mitigate this contrast between faith and experience; it is rather emphasized as strongly as possible in the hope of provoking Jahveh to anger and making Him rise up in wrath against the foes. This explains the practice of placing in strong contrast Hymns extolling Jahveh's grace and power and poems emphasizing His present wrath and apparent impotence.

As we shall see later, the individual poems exhibit the same passionateness, and in many cases the same complete despair. Some pious men, however, were able to renounce all their keen personal desires. The Jew can attain to self-renunciation, but he has never been able to abandon his hope for his people !

Another characteristic feature deserves special mention. The thought of Israel's *sin* hardly ever appears in the National Dirges; indeed, it is frequently disclaimed. Especially in the later period we find a clear consciousness of fidelity to the Law.

This reveals one aspect of the national religion. A second aspect presents a strong contrast to it. The Hymns extol God's grace and faithfulness in the present and His wonderful works in past days. Faith found solace in recalling the distant past, because it found there the wonderful works it failed to see in its own day. And in the narratives dealing with these past times the note of penitence was heard, although it was more on account of the sins of the fathers rather than of their own. Cf. Ps. cvi.

Among the Psalms there are also National Songs of

Praise, originally sung to celebrate great national deliverances, but they are very few. " Full oft they have afflicted me from my youth, yet they have not prevailed against me " (Ps. cxxix). " Round about Jerusalem are mountains, and Jahveh is round about His people " (Ps. cxxv). " Blessed be Jahveh, who hath not abandoned us to their teeth " (Ps. cxxiv). Or in the individual songs we hear the pilgrim singing as he enters Jerusalem of the splendours of the Holy City (Ps. cxxii), so that it is not always the note of lamentation and woe that we hear. The religious passionateness had its moments of relaxation. But even these poems are never without aspirations, although lamentation is occasionally absent, and the dominant note of the Jewish mind, when bent on the history of the nation, is that of grief.

But faith can also shake off despair, and we see it achieving this in the " eschatological psalms." These poems, which treat of the blessed latter days, follow both in form and in content the pattern of the prophets and the prophecies of salvation. The same pattern is also found at the conclusion of the messages of the prophets of woe. In imitation of these writers the Psalmists depict Jahveh's future appearing and repeat His exhortations in the form of a prophetic Word of Judgment (Ps. lxxxii). Or, again imitating prophetic example, they give in anticipation the Hymn which the delivered nation shall one day sing (Ps. cxlix). Or they sing already of the glory of the holy place where the great deed of Jahveh shall be accomplished (Pss. xlvi, xlviii, lxxvi). Or they adopt the style of a Royal Song, such as was chanted when a king ascended the throne, and transfer it to Jahveh's future reign (Ps. xcvii). Psalmists can dare thus to assume the predictive mantle of the prophets, because they also lay claim to Divine

THE RELIGION OF THE PSALMS

inspiration—belief in the inspiration of the minstrel is universal throughout the ancient world. Now and again we find similar eschatological hopes even in the Individual Dirges, especially when certainty of being heard is at its zenith. This shows how deep the hope of Israel's future lay in the individual religious heart. Judaism lives on this expectation, and no pious heart can live without it.

In the substance of their prophecies the Psalmists agree on the whole with their prophetic models, but there are also some significant variations.

This hope is the deep-felt answer to the lamentations and questionings of the National Dirge. It is the expression of the immovable courage of faith, of unshaken confidence. That on which your hearts are set, that for which you have longed with floods of tears, shall be when the time is come! *And this time is at hand!* This word " soon," " at hand," is an integral part of all prophecy of salvation, and is an indication of the zest with which this future was yearned for.

All woe shall soon be ended! Not for ever shall the sceptre of the wicked rule the inheritance of the righteous. Not for ever shall Jerusalem lie in ruins and Israel be dispersed in exile. The time is coming when Jahveh shall rebuild the city and lead His people home. They who now sow in tears shall reap in joy!

Then will begin *Jahveh's dominion*. Amid shouts of joy He ascends to heaven and sits down on the throne of the world, above the cherubim. Heaven and earth now lie at His feet, and the nations greet with exultations the new King.

Then, too, ceases the *dominion of the gods*. They fall down before Jahveh and all who served them are put to shame. God steps into the midst of their assembly, in which they were wont to settle the affairs of the world, and addresses them with indignant words : " Ye were established as sons of the Highest, but ye have wickedly exceeded your authority. Now shall ye die, as if ye were nothing but men " (Ps. lxxxii). In this manner the poet, borrowing a fanciful picture from mythology, describes the victory of the one true God over the many gods of the earth.

At that day, too, *the dominion of the heathen* is broken. Those who once impudently rose against Jahveh must now learn to fear Jahveh's name. They gather themselves together to serve Him and bring Him tribute. Then also *the truth of religion* is demonstrated. The eyes of men shall see that Jahveh is the true God and Israel His chosen people. The poor sufferers will rejoice when they see that Jahveh is Supreme above all gods, and when the scorners who formerly mocked God and His people have to admit that " Jahveh hath done great things for them." When God is thus glorified, His people share in the glory. When God becomes the Monarch of the world, He gives to Israel the dominion of the world. They march to the holy war, bathe their feet in the blood of the wicked, and celebrate the wondrous victory with songs of praise on their lips and two-edged swords in their hands (Ps. cxlix).

This hope comprises all that the Hebrew heart desires : deliverance from the power of the heathen, revenge for the violence they have suffered, the dream of world dominion, the deep-felt longing for righteousness on earth and for the revelation of Jahveh, the desire for the triumph of the true God over His heathen rivals. Political, moral, social, and religious elements are all brought here into a unity. But all the gracious gifts looked for by the nation at that day are summed up in the words "Jahveh will turn the crisis of Israel," i.e. He will establish Israel as it was at the first. Both those who announce this message and those who hear it have their hearts filled with religious enthusiasm, delight, and gratitude.

Hebrew national piety thus oscillates between two extremes, the woe of the present and ardent hope for the future. Both are felt with equal passionateness and equal inevitableness. Any account of Hebrew religion must exhibit the two side by side. This was felt by Psalmists who gave voice to liturgies consisting of heartfelt prayers answered by descriptions of the joy of the last times, or, in a different arrangement, consisting of pictures of the future interrupted by the sighs of the people.

> When Jahveh one day turns
>   the 'fate' of Zion
>   we are as in a dream!
> Then is our mouth
>   full of laughter
>   our tongue with jubilation.
> Then they say among the heathen:
>   Jahveh has done
>   great things for them!
> Jahveh has done
>   great things for us:
>   therefore are we glad!

Then comes the answer of the congregation. None of the things triumphantly foretold by the prophet have yet come to pass. Jahveh, accomplish it speedily!

> Turn, Jahveh, our fate
>   like streams in the south.
> They who sow in tears reap with joy!
> The husbandman goes in tears
>   and scatters the seed;
> Home he will come rejoicing
>   bearing the sheaves.

The beauty of such a poem consists in the success with which the poet has expressed with equal perfection the two aspects of religion—the lament of the nation and the hope of the prophets.

In estimating the Jewish hope, two things must be distinguished: first, the demand for justice and righteousness in the world, and for the punishment of the wicked, as well as the longing to see the presence of God, who has kept silence so long—that is a genuine Advent spirit, intelligible also to a Christian heart; and second, the feverish dream of a tortured people to be permitted one day, in spite of all they have gone through, to play the leading part among the nations—that is a Jewish national desire, which has no appeal for Christians.

In seeking an explanation of the details, it is important to remember that the hopes of the Psalmists are tinged with elements that were originally mythological. Of course, that is no part of their religion; it belongs rather to their poetic fancy. It should further be noticed that, in distinction from many of the prophets, the Psalmists nowhere make mention of *the Messiah*. The King, whose dominion is longed for, is Jahveh Himself. Here the Psalms follow a definite prophetical direction, with which we are familiar in Deutero-Isaiah (chapters xl ff.). On the other hand, we hear much about the King in the so-called Royal Psalms, where we make acquaintance with the religion of the royal Court.

3. THE RELIGION OF THE ROYAL COURT.

The Royal Psalms have preserved a place in the Psalter because post-exilic times interpreted them as referring to the Messiah. Later scholars, who did not know what to make of this interpretation, sought to replace it by others equally untenable. It is only in recent times that acquaintance with similar Egyptian and Babylonian poems has made it clear beyond all doubt that the Biblical poems of this kind refer to the king who occupied the throne in the poet's day. There is absolutely no reason for interpreting them as referring to any other than the pre-exilic monarchy. Most of the Royal Psalms may quite well belong to the last days of the Kingdom of Judah.

Most of them are clearly connected with the varied royal celebrations which were held at the king's Court, especially the royal Court at Jerusalem. Every royal Court feels the need of festivities to enable it to " bear the tedium of life and the unspeakable monotony of the days."[1] But the festivities presupposed in the Psalms are partly of a *religious* nature. That holds good not only of Israel. For us, too, the national State is one of the highest moral possessions of our nation. We, too, pray God to preserve it; and it seemed a natural thing to every nation of antiquity that its king, when it had one, should stand in a specially close relation to the deity. The Court itself also cultivated this relation in order that the deity might defend the monarch in his dangerous elevation. Such religious celebrations were of many kinds. When the young king ascended the throne a great celebration was held, and a herald announced to all the world, " He has become king." The anniversaries of his accession or of his birth were also occasions of rejoicing. In Jerusalem there was another festival to commemorate the founding of the dynasty and the building of the sanctuary. The two were one, for David, the ancestor of the dynasty, was also the founder of the holy place. Another occasion for festivity was the king's marriage, and another was

[1] Schiller, *Die Braut von Messina*.

the time when he went forth to war, and still another when he returned safe, crowned with victory. And although no examples actually occur in the Psalter, we may surely infer that there were days of lamentation when the king fell sick, and services of thanksgiving when he was restored to health.

On all these occasions songs were sung, and these are the Royal Psalms. We are to think of them as sung in presence of the king and his Court in the sanctuary by the singers of the royal choir. On the day of the king's accession the choir sang " He reigneth," and at a later time this was sung with reference to Jahveh (Ps. xcvii). Or the choir announced in the king's name his principles of government in which the whole people should rejoice (Ps. ci). Or at such a celebration the divine Oracle spoke (Ps. cx), occasionally from the king's own lips (Ps. ii). Praises and congratulations were expressed on the anniversary of his accession or on his birthday (Pss. xxi, lxxii, xlv). When the king went forth to war a singer prayed for and promised the help of Jahveh (Ps. xx); when he returned from the campaign a song of thanksgiving was sung (Ps. xviii). On the day when the sanctuary was founded a liturgy was rendered, giving first a dramatic account of how David brought the ark of the Lord to Zion, and then a prophecy that Jahveh would bless David and his house (Ps. cxxxii).

These royal poems are distinguished by a tone of great extravagance: everlasting life is promised to the king—

>   He shall reign ' as long as ' the sun shall shine
> (Ps. lxxii. 5),

as well as world dominion—

>   He shall reign from sea to sea,
>   From the river to the ends of the earth.
> (Ps. lxxii. 8.)

THE RELIGION OF THE PSALMS 91

In order to understand such words we must know that they are imitations of Egyptian and Babylonian royal songs. In the great rulers of the world empires the petty king of Judah saw exalted types of himself, and much that sounded quite natural on the lips of foreign poets—such as the promise of world dominion—sounds somewhat unreal when carried over to the conditions in Judah.

A similar extravagance marks the *religious elements* in these Psalms, but we must again bear in mind the influence of foreign models, and we must further remember that the poet is not describing any one actual king, but has in his mind a royal ideal whom he identifies with his own monarch.

The main religious ideas of these songs are as follows: All the glory that surrounds the king comes from God —all that he actually now possesses and all the promise that the future holds for him. Jahveh has anointed him with the oil of joy and placed the crown of gold upon his head. It is Jahveh who gives him immortality and deathless glory. Scenes of battle are described in which God marches at the king's side and inspires the nations with fear before Him. But however highly the Court poet may laud the monarch, he never forgets that Jahveh is high above the king. The great song of the victory that is promised in Ps. xxi. 6 is not meant to extol the king, but to proclaim the glory of the deity who has helped him.

We hear much of the *close relation in which the monarch stands to his God.* He is under Jahveh's special protection; he is called His Consecrated One, His Anointed One. Priesthood is also ascribed to him, and, as in the case of the Babylonian and Egyptian rulers, great stress is laid on this. The king occupies the seat of honour on Jahveh's right hand. He is called His Son.

In one passage, indeed, although the most recent expositors will not admit this, he is called God:

> Thy throne, O God   is for ever and ever.
> (Ps. xlv. 7.)

Here again we must keep in view the foreign model. In the world empires the rulers are worshipped as gods or as actual sons of the gods. But there is only one passage in our text of the Psalms where we find this monarch called a god. On all other occasions this extreme is avoided. When the king of Judah is called by Jahveh His "Son," the poet means an adopted, not a begotten, son: "Thou art my son, *to-day* have I begotten thee." These words were without any doubt the regular formula of adoption, and "to-day" here means "the day of thy accession."

It is also a part of the glorification of the king that his *trust in God* and his *justice* are extolled. The dominion of the world is his, because he regards the poor; and victory, because he is on the side of the right; his deliverance from all enemies is due to his justice. Here again it should be kept in view that the poet is describing his ideal. The true king is good and just; that is the poet's deep conviction, and he straightway adds, "Thou art he." Sometimes we can even read between the lines a word of exhortation or admonition which the poet dare not expressly utter; for instance, when he prays for the king, "Jahveh, give the king Thy judgments, that He may judge Thy people with righteousness" (Ps. lxxii. 1 f.); or when he puts into the king's lips a promise to surround himself only with righteous and worthy men, and to banish from his Court all slanderers and evil-doers. This is again an

THE RELIGION OF THE PSALMS 93

ideal of royalty and an attempt to tame the unruly lion brood of the house of David (Ps. ci).

On the whole, judged by our standards, the religion of the Court is largely "Byzantine," but when compared with the Court songs of all the other ancient nations of the East it is much more moderate and sane.

4. THE RELIGION OF THE INDIVIDUAL.

Our chief sources for this aspect of Hebrew religion are the individual dirges and songs of praise and the proverbial poetry in the Psalter and elsewhere.

Properly speaking, the Psalms which present this aspect of religion are the chief part of the Psalter. In the first place, they constitute the majority of the Psalms, and secondly, they even found their way into the worship of the royal temple. They include a few which deal with individual religion and to which has been added a prayer of intercession for the king. Examples are Pss. lxi and lxxxiv. Such poems of personal religion were so popular and contained such an appeal to every sensitive heart that they were felt to deserve a place even in the worship of the royal temple. Thirdly, in some psalms certain aspects of personal religion have been carried over and applied to *Israel*. Take Ps. cxxix. 1: "'Many a time have they afflicted me from my youth up,' let Israel now say." What has happened in such a case is this. Poems dealing with personal matters really touch the heart quite differently than do those which treat of national sufferings and hopes. Because of this, poems of personal religion were far better developed than those dealing with national religion, and national religion readily borrowed much from the other. The gravest error made by students of the Psalms is that they have completely misunderstood this personal poetry and have taken the living " I," which means the poet himself, as a mere figure of speech meaning the " people."

Let us again look at the origin of these poems and the situation in which they arose, and let us begin with the *Dirges*.

When a man has been afflicted with sickness he repairs to the sanctuary in order to receive there through an act of religion the healing he craves. He performs certain ceremonies, such as washings, or submits to them at other hands, or he offers various sacrifices. He hopes by so doing to obtain an oracle promising future healing. The presupposition underlying such ceremonies is that sickness, especially those forms of it which seriously endanger life, comes from higher powers. To understand this belief we must remember that antiquity was utterly unable to recognize any natural cause of illness and that this made it all the more terrible. In Israel also, in the earliest period, illness was sometimes ascribed to curses which wicked enemies had pronounced. Usually, however, and at a later time always, it was conceived as coming from Jahveh Himself, who in wrath thus afflicted a man because of his sins. The clearest instance in the Old Testament of a sick man thus afflicted of God was Job. But whatever might have been the cause and origin of an illness, it was to Jahveh alone that a man looked for healing.

It was an essential part of the religious ceremony performed by the sick man at the sanctuary that he should utter his prayer for healing in a song. That this is the origin of the Dirges in the Psalter is clear from various allusions still preserved to us, such as

Pss. li. 9, v. 4, and is corroborated by the numerous similar Babylonian dirges with which we are acquainted.

The counterpart to this dirge song is found in the *Song of Thanksgiving* sung by the sick man after he has been healed. When a man had been delivered from serious illness or from grave danger, he came to the holy place and offered the sacrifice which he had promised to bring. A small, or, if his means allowed of it, a large feast was held, in which his friends and acquaintances joyfully took part. At such a festivity a psalm was sung, and it was in this way that these Songs of Thanksgiving arose.

In these two types—the Dirge and the Song of Praise—we find the two main currents of personal religious poetry. Of the two, the former is by far the more important and the more developed. This need not surprise us. It is in keeping with what we know of human nature. Misery is far more deeply felt than the duty of gratitude.

The two types have passed through almost the same history. Originally sung by the sick man or by the man who had received healing, at a later time they were sung or composed in connection with other misfortunes or deliverances. The original occasion of them is still apparent in the metaphors of illness and cure that continued to be used. In the Laments scattered throughout the Book of Jeremiah, the prophet's " illness " is the fact that his prophecies remain unfulfilled, and in many of the Psalms it is difficult to say whether the " sickness " mentioned is literal or metaphorical.

Another, and an extremely important part of the history of both types, is that they passed *from use in the sanctuary into the Hebrew home*. This took place more completely with the Dirges than with the Songs of

Thanksgiving. In the case of the former, the original atmosphere of public worship is hardly ever perceptible in pronounced form—it has to be supplied by the reader. In the Songs of Praise, the atmosphere of public worship is present even in our text, but here also there are songs which deliberately omit all mention of thank-offering, and which merely show us the grateful worshipper in the sanctuary singing his song of praise. This stage of development of the types exhibits a very important change in the nature of religion. In a former time sacrifices and ceremonies were indispensable to give expression to the spiritual life; in the after time religion has freed itself from this need and become, to some extent at least, independent of these external aids. The religious mind begins to hold the external acts in less esteem. The sufferer is convinced that he receives his healing without any intervention of the priest, through God's word alone, and the man who has experienced deliverance knows something that is far better than animal sacrifice. The song of a grateful heart, giving the glory to God, is far more pleasing to Him.

It is the *prophetical spirit* that finds expression in this change in religious thought. The prophets had waged war against sacrifices and ceremonies, demanding true religion and moral uprightness, and it is therefore to their influence that we owe the new teaching in these psalms. This change was of epoch-making importance. The Psalms would never have become models for our own prayers if, like the Babylonian psalms, they had continued to be bound up with all kinds of performances. The pious heart found courage to express to God directly its inmost joys and sorrows. This emergence of a completely personal religion is one

THE RELIGION OF THE PSALMS

of the greatest things to which the Old Testament bears witness.

It is because of this that these personal songs are more precious to us than the songs of public worship. We have to excise and omit a great deal from the latter before we can use them for our own needs. Many of the former—though not all—we can make our own as they stand. They are the Psalter within the Psalter.

It is a characteristic fact that it is in *songs of suffering* that the spiritual life finds strongest expression. This is true of all higher life, especially of religious life. It is human need that leads men to God. When the afflicted man sees that none other can help him, then from the depths of his misery he lifts his hands to God on high. That is why most of the personal songs are songs of troubled hearts.

But why is it that there were so many sufferers in those days ? The answer can be read in the way in which the Psalmists describe themselves. They call themselves the poor, the afflicted, the downtrodden, the humble, the quiet in the land. They complain of oppression at the hands of the rich, the powerful, the proud, and the insolent. It is implied that the poor are the good and that the rich and the mighty have no regard for God. *The poor and the rich are contrasted as constituting two different religious parties.* Such conditions are familiar to us from the Gospels and from Jewish life in the Greek period, when the powerful and the wealthy sided with the ruling nations and adopted their civilization, while the humble people clung to the religion of their fathers. In all probability the same was the case in the Persian period, for Ezra and Nehemiah opposed the mixed marriages and disloyalty of the upper classes, including the high-priestly families. But similar conditions must have prevailed at an earlier time. Jeremiah calls himself one of the " poor " (Jer. xx. 13). Wickedness and indifference to the ancestral religion came in along with foreign civilization. The wealthy classes were in constant danger of deserting to the dominant nation. But at that very time there arose among the poor and the oppressed a more heartfelt religion. In every Jewish village there were bitter, passionate feuds between these two parties, and it was among the poor and the despised that the dirge psalms arose.

This division of the Jewish people into two parties—those who believed in Jahveh and those who had apostatized—was of great importance for the history of religion. Such an inward cleavage always takes place when a national religion, to which all members of the nation belong, is replaced by a deeper religion which lays less emphasis on the mere fact of membership in the nation and attaches more importance to faith and character. Parseeism provides another example of the same phenomenon.

We shall now describe briefly the *religious content* of these poems, taking first the Dirges.

Like the National Dirges, these personal lamentations invariably begin with *an appeal to the Divine name*. That is the appropriate beginning of all prayers, and the practice goes back to the oldest prehistoric period. In view of the general belief that there were many gods and many lords, it was necessary to mention expressly the name of the deity one meant to address. Thus the opening words of all prayers contained the name of the deity invoked. But the Lamentations pronounce the name of Jahveh in a special tone. It is with loud cries of lamentation, nay, with a " roar like that of a roaring lion," that they call upon God for aid.

THE RELIGION OF THE PSALMS

The chief elements in the Lamentations are complaint and petition. The *complaint* describes the great misery of the poet, with the intention of calling down Jahveh's pity and touching His heart. The sufferer thus eases his own pain—pouring out his heart before God. These outpourings are therefore extremely passionate and are full of vehement exaggeration. The woe is dwelt upon —usually, however, in very general terms. A very frequent subject of plaint is the danger of death—unless God hasten to intervene the complainer will die. We constantly meet the metaphor of passing down to Sheol. The complainer laments that he is already in the depths, and makes a lavish use of metaphors which are intelligible only when they are taken together and seen to contain the same basal thought. He has already gone down to the pit, the waters have already gone over his head, Sheol has already locked its doors behind him. This metaphor, which has hitherto not been always understood, is a very ancient one. Concerning an unconscious man it was said his soul had left his body and gone down to the realm of the dead, " to the pit " underneath the earth, into the realm of the dark waters of the deep.

A frequent complaint of the Psalmist is that concerning his *enemies*, and here again most of the expressions used are very vague. It is remarkable that these adversaries do not assail the Psalmist by open, evil deeds, but rather by means of wicked words and treacherous acts of persecution. Originally they must have been wicked sorcerers, who attacked a man with dreadful curses and evil machinations. This idea is common in Babylonian poems. But there is little trace of this dread of magic and evil charm in the Biblical Psalms—another great achievement of Hebrew religion. The complaint about magical charms has been replaced by one concerning slanders and deceptions. Numerous passages make it clear that the enemies referred to are the rich and powerful among the Psalmist's own people. In a few passages they are *heathens*, amongst whom the Psalmist is forced to dwell. To what extent personal enmities play a part it is difficult to say. In any case, it is enmity *for the sake of religion* that is most prominent.

We must therefore here recall what has just been said about the strife between the two parties in the nation. The Judaism of the time was divided into two bitterly opposed camps—a condition that finds a parallel in the rivalries of the Jesuits and the Freemasons in Roman Catholic countries. The point in dispute was the question, *how happiness and earthly success were to be attained*. This was the desire of both parties. Even the religiously minded sought after this kind of happiness, health and long life, wealth, numerous children. But it was to God that they looked for all these. They believed confidently that they would flourish like the trees in the sanctuary and bring forth fruit in their old age. For this reason the religious man clung with all his heart to God, in the full expectation that He would shield him in all danger and bring him to a good end. On the other hand, the high and the rich mocked this faith of "the upright in heart." They thought they knew better. There was no God to look down from heaven and watch over the fate of mortals. Therefore the religious man called them "wicked." They pursued their evil ways in secret and committed all kinds of wickedness. Both parties thus equally relied on the result—a genuinely Jewish feature. Each side watched with equal zeal the fate of the other. The result was bound to bring the truth to light. A somewhat similar attitude was adopted by Protestants and Catholics in the Reformation times. They, too, watched the kind of death that overtook friends and foes. Thus, as sometimes happens when a foreign Power holds sway in a country, when ruin overwhelms the powerful, the "righteous" rejoice. Unfortunately, however, it most frequently happens that the faithful worshipper of Jahveh perishes miserably, and in addition to his other sorrows he has to bear the scorn of the "wicked." "He has cast himself on Jahveh; let Him deliver him! Let Him help him, if He really delighteth in him" (Ps. xxii. 9). That is why we find so frequently in the dirge Psalms sickness and scorn conjoined. The Psalmists are tortured by this scorn, because they cannot deny that it seems to be justified. They are deeply distressed to see that actual conditions so frequently contradict their religious faith. In their prayers, therefore, they wrestle not only for their happiness and even for their lives, but also for God and His cause.

Again and again we hear of *slanders* against the psalm-writer. In his wretchedness he is cast out by all. Even amongst his nearest friends he finds no sympathy; even his own parents will have nothing to do with him; everyone treats him like a heinous sinner and only waits for his death. In order to understand this we must take several considerations into account. Vile gossip and slander are the special vices of small communities where people live close together and busy themselves with each other's affairs. In primitive times it must have been quite common for a sick man's friends to desert and disown him. It was the *dread of illness* that made men do so. Parallels are found in the treatment meted out to lepers in the East, and in the fear of the mentally afflicted that is found amongst ourselves to-day. In Judaism this tendency was increased by the *belief in divine retribution*. Even religious men, who had perhaps been disciples of the psalmist sufferer till now, began to doubt his rectitude when he fell into illness or misfortune, and to suspect that he was in reality a wicked man, whose sins God had exposed by sending these sufferings upon him. He could not possibly be a good man. He must be a wicked man, a criminal, indicated as such by God Himself.

Such was the lot of Job, whose friends exhorted him to repentance, instead of comforting him in his misery. Similarly we find the Psalmist bewailing his sufferings and lamenting over the mockery of his enemies and the slanders of his friends.

Along with this we hear the plaint over the *aloofness of God*, the hiding of His face. " My God, my God, why hast Thou forsaken me ? " Thus the Psalmist bewails both his external lot and his abandonment by God. To be convinced of God's grace while sickness overwhelmed him was very difficult for the sufferer in ancient days. He was sure, rather, that his evil condition was the sign of God's anger, or at least of God's desertion of him. *Vice versa*, God's grace and deliverance out of trouble were inseparably connected. The Old Testament believer could only find inward assurance in a favourable external situation. Occasionally, however, we hear in these dirge psalms such true notes of piety as to enable us to believe that the one heartfelt desire of the singer was after all the nearness of God :

> Like a hart that panteth
>   for waterbrooks,
> so panteth my soul,
>   Jahveh, for Thee.

> My soul thirsteth for Jahveh,
>   for the God ' of my life.'
> When shall I come and behold
>   the face of Jahveh?
>
> (Ps. xlii. 2 f.)

These lines show us that, in the psalmist's mind, the distance and nearness of God are still literally associated with the thought of temple worship. Living far from Zion and its magnificent celebrations, dwelling amongst a nation of strangers hostile both to him and his religion, he feels that this local distance is symbolic of his distance from God. We see here a religion which has almost attained to spirituality, but which cannot yet completely dispense with visible symbols.

On the whole, these dirges are very monotonous. Again and again we come upon the same feelings, thoughts, expressions, and metaphors. This is due to the manner in which this literary type arose. These songs are all founded on temple formularies. True, the material is touched by personal emotion, but it cannot be said to be pervaded by it. The individual element appears, but it is still far from being prominent. It is confined to a definite circle of feelings and forms of expression. The poet of the dirge never even gets the length of mentioning his own name. We must, therefore, be cautious about using phrases like "the freedom of the individual," "the place of the individual in religion," as if they had a definite meaning. Most peculiar of all are the Dirges of Jeremiah, in which personal experiences of the prophet's calling are conjoined with the dirge style of poetry. His enemies are the people who refuse to believe his message, and who accuse him of lack of patriotism because of his prophecies of woe. Similar self-reliance characterizes the Lamentations of Job. Here, too, it is a sick man who utters the prayers, but the complaints take a wider range, because the poet is thinking not only of himself, but also of the sufferings of the whole human race, and voices his world pain in the moving words :

> The man that is born of woman
> is of few days and full of trouble.
>
> (Job xiv. 1.)

The book of Job finds a problem here, but we shall deal with that later.

The culminating point of the dirge is the *Prayer or Petition*. This is the purpose, tacit or expressed, of all dirges. The plaint and the prayer alternate with each other, but the arrangement is loose. The content of the prayer corresponds to that of the plaint. " Save me from my distress ; heal my sickness ; let my foes be ashamed ; give me not over to their scorn, but keep Thy word to Thy servant. Bring me again to Zion that I may behold Thy temple. Do judgment upon the wicked." The prayer is marked by passionate urgency, as if it would take God by storm. That other prayer, " Father, not as I will, but as Thou wilt," is on a quite different level. The petitioner in the dirge claims to know what God *must* do. He seeks to move God to fulfil *his* will, and his passionateness reaches its climax in his prayer for *vengeance against his adversary*. The idea and ideal of forgiving the adversary are utterly absent. With burning anger, and at times with coarse expressions, he prays for destruction upon his enemies. Even a man like Jeremiah prayed thus ! The so-called imprecatory psalms contain little else than such curses. The psalmist utters these prayers quite frankly, without any thought of concealment, for his enemies are Jahveh's enemies also. "Should I not hate them that hate Thee?" He is convinced that there is nothing unjust in such prayers, for his enemies have richly deserved destruction. Let the evil they have done or purposed return upon their own head.

There are occasions when the psalmist sums up all his desires in one comprehensive figure of speech. He hopes after his recovery to make a pilgrimage to Jerusalem—then he will have attained his heart's desire, healing and nearness to God. And still another thought emerges: the temple is a refuge. No one can hurt the man whom Jahveh covers with protection in His sanctuary, and in the house of the Lord he finds rest from the persecutions of the wicked.

It remains to add that the idea of *life after death appears nowhere in the Psalter*. What the psalmist desires is deliverance from his present danger. This desire is often expressed in passionate language:

> Thou wilt not give my soul to Sheol,
> Thou wilt not let Thy godly one see the pit.
> (Ps. xvi. 10.)

But this does not mean deliverance into a new life beyond death, but a new life before death, a life that to his ardent mind seems an everlasting life:

> Thou wilt shew me the path of life!
> In Thy presence there is fullness of joy,
> In Thy right hand there are pleasures for evermore.
> (Ps. xvi. 11.)

There is another thought that is never found in these psalms, the thought of *education through suffering*. The godly man does not try to bear patiently the chastisements of God; he seeks to be delivered from the ills that come upon him. Job angrily rejects the opinion of his friends that God has sent his sufferings upon him to warn and chasten him. On the other hand, this idea occurs in the psalms of thanksgiving and is quite frequent in the Proverbs.

It is common to find both plaint and prayer supported by all kinds of *motives* in order to induce God to intervene, and by thoughts with which the psalmist comforts and soothes his troubled mind. One of the most frequent is his declaration of immovable confidence in the help of God. Plaint and prayer thus pass into calm confidence and settled assurance. " Many, indeed, say of me, ' Even God can help him no more '; but I believe and I know that Thou, O Lord, art a shield about me. Thou wilt not suffer my honour to be trampled in the dust " (Ps. iii. 3 f.). He finds it soothing thus to declare this confidence, and he hopes that God will not put to shame one that approaches Him thus. God cannot put away from Him hands that cling to Him so confidently. Such trust cannot fail to move His heart. Nor can a brief, humble word of personal experience, justifying such confidence, be out of place: " I was cast upon Thee from my youth up " (Ps. xxii. 11). " Now, in the time of my old age, leave me not " (Ps. lxxi. 9).

Important sub-species of these dirge psalms are the *Psalms of Penitence* and *Songs of Innocence*. In both the psalmist complains of his misery and prays for its removal. The difference between them is that in the former he confesses his sin, while in the latter he maintains his innocence. Both types were originally used in public worship, and Babylonian literature supplies parallels to both.

1 (*a*). The authors of the Psalms of Penitence are convinced that by their sin they have incurred God's

anger, and the purpose of their psalms is to urge God to forgive them. A classical example is Psalm li. The whole content of these psalms must be interpreted in view of their purpose, which is to incline God's heart to mercy. The Psalmist, e.g., reminds God of the universality of human sin, so that his own sinfulness may not appear so grievous:

> I was brought forth in sin,
> in guilt did my mother conceive me
> (Ps. li. 7),

that is to say: "From an unclean man, in whom sin is inborn, Thou canst not demand perfection." Again, he confesses his sin with the utmost frankness, humbling himself before the Most High, having in mind the thought:

> God scorneth the scorners,
> But He giveth grace to the humble.
> (Prov. iii. 34.)

He who sincerely acknowledges his sin can expect forgiveness; he who conceals it must be punished, till his obstinacy is broken. But the deepest prayer in the penitential psalms is that for a new and clean heart (Ps. li. 12), a prayer that stands far above all other prayers in the psalter. Elsewhere we find prayers for external possessions, for life and prosperity, even for instruction regarding the way of righteousness and for guidance to do the right. All these assume that man himself can and should fulfil the will of God. But in this profound prayer the thought emerges that goodness in man must be the work of God. This is the culmination of the religion of the Psalms. Here it transcends itself.

1 (b). There is one essential feature in which the

Songs of Innocence present a contrast to these Penitential Psalms. In the former also the psalmist inquires for the cause of his sufferings, but he cannot find it in himself, for there is no sin in him. The characteristic and ever recurrent feature of these poems is that the psalmist strongly asserts his innocence :

>   Thou provest my heart   Thou testest it in the night,
>   Thou triest me ;   Thou findest no evil thing in me.
>   (Ps. xvii. 3.)

Such declarations of innocence, lofty in style, are frequent in the book of Job, but when the author of such a song finds absolutely no reason for his misfortune in his own sin, he cries all the more loudly to God for help, and his passion is poured out in full strength upon his adversaries. Psalms of Vengeance and Songs of Innocence belong together.

We to-day are inclined to set a higher value on the Penitential Psalms, with their confessions of sin, than on the Songs of Innocence, with their insistence on self-righteousness. But perhaps this judgment is not altogether just and right. In the psalmists' day it was not difficult for men in their distress to speak of their sin. Babylonian prayers contain many such confessions, all of them evidently superficial and insincere. But a more manly and more courageous attitude is sometimes that of the man whose spirit is not broken by misfortune and who maintains the conviction of his innocence. The moral greatness to which such a man may rise is seen in Job, sublime in his defiance of misfortune.

In the Songs of Innocence there is very frequent reference to *Divine Retribution*. This tenet of Hebrew faith has already been mentioned, but we must now deal with it more fully.

THE RELIGION OF THE PSALMS 109

This doctrine is not found in the oldest dirges. The earlier religion was satisfied with the faith that Jahveh cannot abandon His loyal servants. But by and by reflection entered more largely into lyric poetry. The Dirge and the Wisdom literature—originally distinct and separate—coalesced, and it was in the latter that the doctrine of Retribution was discussed. Then the religious mind, to assure itself of divine help, fell back on the basal principle of divine dealing, and found refuge in the thought that God deals well by those that fear Him. Ultimately, this principle became the guiding line of piety, and appeared even in the Religion of the Psalms.

This doctrine is usually found in the form of The Blessing. "Happy is the man who walketh in the way of the Lord. He shall be like a tree planted by the waterbrooks" (Pss. i and cxxviii). Occasionally a high degree of individualism is found. "Though a thousand fall at thy right hand and ten thousand at thy left hand, it shall not come nigh thee" (Ps. xci. 7). It even finds vent in the form of Exhortation (Ps. xxxvii). At a still later time the suffering saint consoled himself with the same thoughts in his dirge.

Sometimes, but only rarely, the theme is *what God requires of man*. This also takes the form of The Blessing (Ps. i), or of a Hymn to the Law (Ps. xix. 8–11). Psalm l gives a solemn exposition of the Law in a manner reminiscent of the prophets. The Psalms contain little that indicates any high estimate of the legal ceremonies, and Psalm l strongly repudiates zeal for the Law apart from morality of life. The relationship between God and man in the Psalms is, as everywhere in the Old Testament, including the prophets, that of the Law—God commands and man must obey, receiving in return protection and reward. Any important influence of the great legal systems, such as became clearly apparent in later Judaism, is entirely absent from the Psalms.

The doctrine of Retribution has lost much of its certainty for the authors of the later dirges. When they see how things really are in the world, how the wicked blaspheme God and yet enjoy prosperity, they are seized with dread and ask, Is there really an avenging God? The psalmists who tackle this problem find consolation in the hope that divine judgment will ultimately fall upon the workers of wickedness (Pss. xxxvii and lxxiii).

Almost all the dirges end on a note of triumph. Glad certainty finally fills the psalmist's heart. Out of his plaint, even out of his despair, he rises to the assurance that God will aid him. This inward assurance is the answer to his prayer.

This assured confidence comes so suddenly that many psalms seem to fall into two entirely separate parts. Indeed, some modern scholars would call these parts two independent poems. Psalm xxii is an example. But this view leaves out of account the passionateness of Hebrew prayer. It is possible, however, that the two parts, when sung originally, were separated by the announcement of the priestly oracle.

The usual form of the conclusion is that the psalmist makes a vow to sing a song of thanksgiving after his deliverance has come and sings this song in anticipation of it. And so the dirge, which began with cries and tears, ends with thanksgiving and praise.

We saw previously that the national religion oscillated between two extremes: sorrow and joy, the dirge and the eschatological poem. The same is true of the personal religion in the Psalms. Dirge and Song of Thanksgiving are found side by side.

The Songs of Thanksgiving are full of exultation. The whole situation has changed. The former sufferer, now basking in the sunshine of happiness, triumphantly tells his friends of his former griefs and recounts how God heard his cry. They see in him, with joy and pride, a proof that God does not abandon His faithful worshippers. While the individual dirges are sung in privacy, the song of thanksgiving is meant to be heard by all. The most sacred duty of the man to whom deliverance has come is to give the glory to God, and to testify aloud of God's goodness so that all the world may hear.

The Songs of Thanksgiving are an exact contrast to the Dirges—the obverse of the coin—and thus they interpret each other. To take one example: the dirge-singer laments, "I am swallowed up by the pit"; he prays, "Lord, save my life from the pit"; he concludes with the vow, "I will praise Thee, when Thou hast raised me from the pit." On the other hand, the man who has been delivered opens his Song of Praise by recounting his distress and his deliverance. "I had been swallowed up of Sheol, but Thou didst save my life from the pit." And the Song concludes: "I bless Thee that Thou hast raised me from the pit." This comparison is another proof that the prayer for deliverance from death does not envisage a life after death, but help in the present danger.

This alternation between the Dirge and the Song of Thanksgiving covers the entire religious life. In need a man calls on God; when happiness returns he gives God praise. The glowing passionateness of the Hebrew mind, of which we have repeatedly spoken, explains why the religion is full of such contrasts.

All the greater is the value we attach to the exceptions. There are passages in the dirges in which the poet declares his *confidence in God*. The tone is that of calm assurance. The tumult has been stilled and quiet confidence fills the heart:

> Jahveh is my light and salvation
>   Of whom shall I be afraid?
> Jahveh is the strength of my life,
>   whom shall I fear?
>
> (Ps. xxvii. 1.)

The poems in which these two moods find voice simultaneously are true to life and touch us deeply. Examples are Psalms iii, cxxiii, cxxx. It is a majestic picture that the author of the splendid verses in Psalms xliii and xliv unveils, conjoining deep grief, gnawing pain, powerful pleading, remembrance of a happier past with confident certainty. Especially beautiful is a poem like Psalm cxxi, in which the poet reads off his varying emotions. There are a few psalms in which plaint and prayer have completely ceased and only confidence finds expression. "The Lord is my shepherd, I shall not want" (Ps. xxiii). These Songs of Trust, in which the passionate, ardent Hebrew has disciplined his heart's restlessness to peace, are to us the finest individual poetry in the psalter. But perhaps the finest verse in all the Psalms is that which a poet, after a painful debate with his own heart concerning the prosperity of the wicked and his own sufferings, has found the grace to say:

> If only I have Thee,
>   nought else in heaven and earth do I desire:
> Though body and soul pine away,
>   Thou art still my heart's comfort and portion.
>
> (Ps. lxxiii. 25.)

5.

It is a mere outline of the Religion of the Psalms that I have been able to give. Only some specially frequent notes of this religion and a few simple aspects of it have been referred to. The contents of the Psalms is far richer and more copious. Especially in the later period, when the poetical types became more and more literary, much coalescence took place and the structure became more complicated. The poet's joy in his deliverance is tinged by the recollection of his need, and he now indites the dirge which he sang in his distress (Jonah ii. 5). Or the dirge adopts hymn material and exhibits the strong contrast between human sorrow and God's glory as a means for opening the heart of God (Ps. xxii. 4–6). Or it describes the transitoriness of human life (a dirge *motif*) in order to make more manifest the eternity of God (Ps. ciii. 15 f.). Other examples of coalescence are found in the "liturgy," where passages of varied character are conjoined for use in the sanctuary. In this way the religion became richer as time went on.

Ultimately naïve religion was invaded by a rational reflection which finally destroyed it. That is what we have in Psalm cxix and in the post-canonical Psalms of Solomon.

In this lecture I have tried to give in as unbiased a manner as I could the results of my studies in the Psalms. While I have not concealed the weak points in the religion, I have tried to bring out its strength. Such a study may justifiably be concluded by an impartial and understanding verdict on the value of the Psalms, and I should like briefly to indicate the opinion I have formed. On the one hand, it is utterly impossible for us now to use the entire Psalter in Christian worship, although earlier times may have so used it. The modern mind has found in it so much that is alien and even repellent that we have long been compelled to make selections for use in church and school and home. On the other hand, we should be careful not to go too far in this direction. We must remember that the Psalter is not a book of to-day, and therefore cannot possibly voice modern thoughts and feelings. The layman, who seeks religious edification in this book, will do well simply to pass over what to him is meantime unintelligible and strange; further experience of life will perhaps cast a different light upon it. And a modern woman, who is of yesterday and will disappear to-morrow, would do well to preserve a reverent silence concerning a book that has influenced so many centuries. Whoever earnestly studies these poems will not fail to find many passages which give perfect expression to true religion, and generations still to come will humbly bend the knee on this holy ground and learn from the Hebrew psalmists how to pray.

IV

THE CLOSE OF MICAH: A PROPHETICAL LITURGY

A STUDY IN LITERARY HISTORY [1]

THE purpose of this essay is to give a plain example of the modern method of Bible study from the point of view of literary history. The passage to be discussed has therefore not been chosen on account of any special religious value or æsthetic beauty, nor because of any specially striking results that will be reached. It has been selected for discussion here simply because the treatment of this passage permits an easy demonstration of the method above mentioned.

This kind of study is still comparatively new in Old Testament scholarship, and it is therefore not surprising that, like every other new thing, it has given rise to all sorts of misunderstandings. We shall therefore begin by stating clearly what is meant by it. The Literary History of the Bible analyses the lyrical and prophetical writings of the Old Testament—it is only with these that we are concerned here—into their native " types." We classify into such types those passages which have in common a definite content of thoughts and feelings. That is the first step. A second distinctive feature of a type is a pronounced literary style—the constant recurrence of ways of expression, phrasings, words, metaphors,

[1] First printed in *Zeitschrift für Semitistik*, edited by F. Littmann, vol. ii, 1924, pp. 145 ff.

etc. Great importance is attached to these, because they afford a very easy means of identifying the type. Again, and this is specially true of the lyric poetry, these types had originally a definite "place in the life" of Israel. One of the most important objects of this method of study is to exhibit the rise and growth of the entire written literature of Israel on the basis of this investigation of literary types, and the same method should also be carried into the exposition of individual passages. In expounding a passage we must first determine by an examination of the characteristics just mentioned to what literary type it belongs, and perhaps even what place it occupies in the history of the type in question. This matter of the type is of great, sometimes of fundamental, importance, because we thus are guided to other passages which provide absolutely certain parallels, and the meaning of many a passage which at first sight is obscure becomes clear when we see its kinship with other passages, which may be far distant from it in the pages of the Bible. Difficulties of interpretation disappear, and we also gain a new means for the emendation of corruptions in the text. These considerations are sufficient to show that this line of investigation is not, as has recently been alleged, mainly occupied with folk-lore and æsthetics, with matters of literary form and taste. Nor does its chief interest lie in discovering parallels in other literatures. Its purpose is, on the basis of reliable study of the Bible itself, to promote a better understanding of the Old Testament.

Another point concerning the form of this essay may be mentioned here. When dealing with such matters, Historical Science moves in a constant circle. From separate details it deduces a general rule, and immediately uses this rule to interpret the separate details.

THE CLOSE OF MICAH

This is the inevitable method for the study of the Literary History of Israel. It involves, however, this difficulty for the exponent of the method, that while he may find it easy to indicate in the text with which he is dealing the various details, he cannot with equal brevity bring out in connection with it the general rule which he has deduced from other cases. Such an essay as this, therefore, can only be an invitation to the theological reader to undertake similar investigations for himself. The wider, more general statements will be understood only by a student who is willing to study in this way not only one single passage, but numerous passages, and to devote not only one short hour, but many hours, to this method of investigation.

I.

Our first passage, Micah vii. 7–10, is as follows :

7. ' ' I will look out for Jahveh [1]	3
I will wait for the God of my salvation,	
my God will hear my prayer.	3 + 2
8. Exult not over me, foe of mine [2]	
although I am down, I shall rise.	3 + 2
Though I sit in darkness,	
Jahveh abides my light.	2 + 2
9. Jahveh's anger I will bear,	
for I sinned against Him,	3 + 2
until He fights my fight	
and pleads my cause ;	3 + 2
He brings me out to the light,	
I see His righteousness.	2 + 2

---

[1] Omit *vav* at the beginning. Single inverted commas indicate changes of text. Roman numerals between single commas indicate the number of words omitted. The numerals on the right are the numbers of metrical feet. [2] The word is feminine.

10. My foe[1] shall see it,
    Shame shall cover her   2 + 2
who says now to me : Where is He,
    Jahveh, thy God ?   3 + 2
My eyes shall gloat on her ;   3
    now is she trampled
        like dirt of the street.   3 + 2

Just one word on the metrical structure. For the most part the passage is of regular construction. To use Sievers's terminology, it consists of " double fives." But this regularity is broken by a few variations, and here, as in other similar cases, modern scholars have tried to restore complete regularity. It is open to doubt, however, whether such attempts do not do violence to the Hebrew sense for metre, and whether that sense did not demand a certain variety. I have pointed out elsewhere [2] numerous other passages where similar interruptions occur in the midst of " double fives."

With regard to the literary type to which the passage belongs, it is not, strictly speaking, in prophetic style. Its contents are not prophecies, such as are, after all, the most characteristic utterances of the prophets ; the notes we hear in it are lyrical. It is not a prophetic utterance, but a poem. This has been generally admitted. It was pointed out first by Bernhard Stade,[3] whose keen eye recognized its kinship to the Psalms. Owing, however, to the then prevalent opinion that the " I " of the Psalms meant the community and not a person, he did not get so far as to distinguish different types in the Psalter. We know now that this is not the

---

[1] The word is feminine.
[2] See on this subject my *Commentary on the Psalms*, p. 633.
[3] *Zeitschrift für die alttestamentliche Wissenschaft*, xxiii, 1903, p. 164 ff.

only example of a lyric poem appearing in a prophetical book. The lyric was adopted by the prophets at a definite period and for definite reasons. I have tried to describe and explain this fact elsewhere.[1] I have also showed there that the lyrical types used by the prophets, so far as they are of a religious kind, resemble those of the Psalms. What type have we here? One glance at the contents of the passage enables us to answer the question.

The speaker is an " I " who at the moment is in deep distress. " I have fallen," " I must sit in darkness " (verse 8). Jahveh's anger has fallen on this " I " (verse 9). But his deepest pain is that he is oppressed by an enemy (female), who maliciously exults over him (verse 8). " Where is He, Jahveh, thy God ? " (verse 10). The chief content of the passage, however, is a declaration of immovable hope that his lot will change and that he will be brought from darkness into light (verse 9), while the mocking foe will be brought to shame and destruction (verse 10).

To anyone familiar with the literary types of the Psalms, this is sufficient to show that the passage before us is a Dirge or Lamentation. We have here the invariable situation presupposed in the Hebrew Dirge —a suppliant in the midst of distress so great that human aid is unavailing, and we have also the essential contents of the Dirge—an expression of longing and hope that Jahveh Himself will intervene.

This diagnosis is confirmed when we look closer into the poem and try to find parallels among the Lamentations in the Bible. Seeing that our passage speaks of an " I," we shall first compare it with the Individual Dirges.

[1] See introductory essays to Hans Schmidt's *Die Grossen Propheten*, 2nd ed., p. lvi ff.

The chief portion of the poem—verses 8–10—is a dispute with a malicious enemy. Exult not too loudly over my sad downfall, my present gloomy lot. You think this condition will last for ever, but your exultation is premature. A change is coming which will silence your arrogant lips. Though I am down, I shall rise; and even now in my darkness my confidence is unshaken that Jahveh will bring me into the light (verse 8). Then follows a parenthetic reflection. My hope may not be fulfilled in the immediate future. The time of divine wrath is upon me still, and as it is not undeserved I must bear it with resignation. But immediately the longing and the hope start into flame again. God's anger against me will cease one day, and I await quietly the hour when Jahveh will Himself undertake my cause. Then He will lead me out of my darkness into light, and in His faithfulness I shall see my desire (verse 9). Then, at the close, the whole ardour of the poem is hurled upon the enemy. My deliverance means a change for her too. She, whose mockery is poured upon me and my God, will then be compelled to be a witness of my justification. Shame shall cover her, and all her imaginings will be proved to have been folly. I shall see her deep humiliation, trodden down like dirt in the street, and I shall have my joy in seeing it (verse 10).

It would cause us no surprise if we found most of these thoughts—we shall deal later with the exceptions—in an Individual Dirge in the Psalms. These dirges frequently show their authors in dispute with their adversaries, and exhibit much of the exultation and triumph that we find in this passage. Arrogant men laugh at the psalmist's misery and imagine that they will triumph over him, and this laughter wounds him

THE CLOSE OF MICAH

sorely. "When I halt, they rejoice."[1] He cries, "How long shall mine enemy exult over me?"[2] He pleads, "Let not mine enemy say, 'I have prevailed against him.'"[3] He prays that God would at last take up his cause and deal justly by him. "Let my sentence come from Thee. Let my [4] eyes see justice."[5] Then the longed-for change will come. Prosperity and honour shall be his, while his enemies are doomed to shame and disappointment. "They shall come to shame and dishonour."[6] "Let them be covered with reproach and dishonour."[7] That is one of the most frequent prayers in the Dirge Psalms.[8] And occasionally, as in our passage, this feeling takes the intense form of a prayer that ere all be done the two parties shall be brought face to face, that the enemy may yet see with chagrin the prosperity of the righteous,[9] while the righteous sees with joy the destruction of his persecutors.[10] There is also a frequent recurrence of the thought that while the suppliant acknowledges his sin and bends humbly before the God Who has stricken him, he is also fully conscious that he has been vindicated against his enemy.[11]

Further, *the forms of expression* used in our passage and in the Dirge Psalms are the same. In both we

[1] Ps. xxxv. 15.
[2] Ps. xiii. 2.
[3] Pss. xiii. 5. Cf. xxv. 2; xxxv. 19, 24; xxxviii. 16; xxxix. 8.
[4] Changes in the text are defended in my *Commentary on the Psalms*.
[5] Pss. xvii. 2. Cf. vii. 9; xxxv. 23; xliii. 1; cxix. 154.
[6] Pss. xxxv. 4, 26; xl. 15 f.; lxx. 3 f.; lxxi. 13.
[7] Pss. lxxi. 13; cix. 29.
[8] Pss. vi. 10; xxxi. 18; cix. 28; cxix. 78; Jer. xvii. 18.
[9] Pss. lxxxvi. 17. Cf. xxiii. 5 (cxii. 10).
[10] Pss. lii. 6; liv. 7; lviii. 10; lix. 10. Cf. xcii. 11; cxii. 8.
[11] Pss. vi; xxv; xxxviii; xxxix; xli. 4 f; cii; and especially lxix.

have the speaker addressing his enemy;[1] the dirge-writer quotes the words which the enemy utters against him and against God,[2] just as verse 10 of our passage quotes the language of the enemy. Indeed, the words here, "Where is he, Jahveh, your God?" are exactly those which the Psalmist hears from the lips of his enemies.[3] In the dirge psalms we read, "Our eyes are turned to Jahveh, our God, *until* He have mercy upon us."[4] Our passage reads, "Jahveh's anger I will bear, *until* He fight my fight." In both the content of the longing is expressed in a sentence beginning with *until*. Again, many of the *words and phrases* are identical. Examples are: the "exulting" of the enemy (verse 8);[5] the word "fall" used for misfortune (verse 8);[6] also the verb "rise" for prosperity (verse 8);[7] "darkness" as a metaphor for misery (verse 8).[8] Jahveh is the "light" of the suppliant (verse 8).[9] "For I sinned against Him" (verse 9).[10] The phrase "to fight my fight" (verse 9) occurs in Ps. xliii. 1 and Ps. cxix. 154, and the word "my cause" (verse 9) in Pss. xvii. 2, xxxv. 23, ix. 4, cxl. 12. To "bring out" in the sense of deliverance (verse 9) is found in Pss. xxv. 15, xxxi. 4, cxliii. 11. Jahveh's righteous, liberating grace (verse 9) is mentioned in Pss. v. 8, xxii. 31, xxxi. 1, xxxv. 24, xxxvi. 10, (xl. 10), li. 14, lxxi. 2, 15, 24, cxix. 40, cxliii. 1.

---

[1] Pss. iv. 2 ff.; vi. 8; lii. 3; lxii. 3; cxix. 115; Psalms of Solomon iv. 1; Job vi. 21 f.; xvii. 10; xix. 2, 21, 28; xxi. 2.
[2] Pss. iii. 2; xi. 1; xxii. 8; xxxv. 21, 25; xlii. 3, 10; lxxi. 11; Jer. xvii. 15; Job xix. 28.
[3] Ps. xlii. 3, 10.
[4] Pss. cxxiii. 2. Cf. cxii. 8.
[5] Cf. Pss. xxxv. 15, 19, 24; xxxviii. 16; (xxx. 1).
[6] Cf. Pss. v. 10; xxvii. 2; xxxvi. 12.
[7] Ps. xxxvi. 12.
[8] Pss. xxxv. 6; lxxxviii. 6; cxliii. 3; Lam. iii. 2, 6.
[9] Ps. xxvii. 1.
[10] Pss. xli. 4; li. 4.

THE CLOSE OF MICAH

This helps us to answer the question whether verse 7 belongs to this poem. Most scholars think it does, although Sellin and Hans Schmidt[1] follow Duhm's view that it is the closing verse of the previous passage. Inquiries of this kind concerning the delimitation of passages have to be reviewed in the light of literary history. The verse expresses the assured hope of the suppliant that his misery will be turned into joy. The previous verse contains a fierce invective, and there is no other example in the prophetic writings of an invective ending with such a declaration of confident trust. The verse fits in far more suitably as part of a dirge.

Phrases like these, "looking out" for Jahveh and "waiting" for His help, find numerous parallels in the Dirges: "I seek Jahveh";[2] "I seek Thy face";[3] "I lift up mine eyes";[4] "I lift up my hands";[5] "I lift up my soul";[6] "I will wait upon Thee";[7] "I spread forth my hands unto Thee";[8] "I have hoped in Thee";[9] "I wait for God";[10] "I trust in God";[11] "I trust in His mercy."[12] The identical phrase used in our passage occurs in Ps. v. 3, "I look for Thee," i.e. for a sacrificial indication promising deliverance. We find also "I hope in Thee";[13] "I wait for the Lord";[14] "I hope in Thy word";[15] "My hope is in Thee alone."[16] In these passages the suppliant calls God, to whom he cleaves in his distress,

---

[1] *Die Grossen Propheten*, 2nd ed., p. 143.
[2] Pss. lxxvii. 3. Cf. lxiii. 2.
[3] Ps. xxvii. 8.
[4] Pss. cxxi. 1; cxxiii. 1.
[5] Ps. xxviii. 2.
[6] Pss. xxv. 1; lxxxvi. 4; cxliii. 8.
[7] Ps. lix. 9.
[8] Pss. lxxxviii. 9; cxliii. 6.
[9] Ps. cxix. 166.
[10] Pss. xxv. 5; cxxx. 5.
[11] Pss. lvi. 11. Cf. xxv. 2; xxxi. 14; lvi. 4; cxliii. 8.
[12] Ps. lii. 8.
[13] Pss. xxxviii. 15. Cf. lxix. 3.
[14] Ps. cxxx. 5 f.
[15] Ps. cxix. 81, 114, 147.
[16] Ps. xxxix. 8.

"my God,"[1] and "the God of my deliverance."[2] The dirge-writers are also fond of mentioning the content of their hope. "The Lord sustaineth me";[3] "He will save me";[4] "He will hear me when I call upon Him";[5] "He answers me."[6] In our passage we have, "My God will hear me" (verse 7). Verse 7 is thus full of dirge phraseology. And it is also worthy of notice that the dirge-writers frequently *begin* their poems with such declarations of trust and longing.[7] The opening word "I" of our passage also occurs as the first word of Lam. iii, "I am the man that hath seen affliction." The same should probably be the case with Psalm lxxiii, where the opening verse in our present text seems to have been prefixed subsequently.[8] This opening with the first personal pronoun was probably adopted from the openings of inscriptions, like that on the Moabite Stone, "I am Mesha," and on Egyptian stele,[9] "I was a man who vowed wickedly." It even reminds us of the manner in which the Babylonian dirge-writers introduce themselves,[10] although they actually begin with a solemn invocation of the deity.[11]

[1] Pss. xxxi. 14; cxl. 6; cxliii. 10.   [2] Pss. xxv. 5; xxvii. 9.
[3] Ps. iii. 5.   [4] Ps. lv. 16.
[5] Ps. iv. 3.   [6] Ps. iii. 4.
[7] Cf. vii. 1; xi. 1; xvi. 1; xxv. 1; xxvii. 1; xxxi. 1; xlii. 1; lxiii. 1; lxxi. 1; cxxi. 1; cxxiii. 1.

[8] Löhr, *Psalmenstudien*, p. 52.

[9] Erman, *Sitzungsberichte der Kgl. Preuss. Akad. der Wissenschaften, Phil.-hist. Cl.*,1911, xlix, p. 1101.

[10] Cf. Stummer, *Sumerische-akkadische Parallelen zum Aufbau alttestamentlicher Psalmen*, p. 68 ff.

[11] The word "and" has been introduced before "I" by a redactor to make a kind of connection with what precedes (Guthe). In reality the two passages have no connection with each other. Additions by a redactor like "and," "for," "therefore" are often found at the beginning of new passages in the prophetical books, For "I" as the opening of Semitic inscriptions, cf. Littmann, *Zur Entzifferung der thalmuden. Inschriften.*

Verse 7 thus really forms an excellent introduction to what follows. It is precisely because the speaker is so confident that God will deliver him that he is able thus early to shout to his enemy, " Exult not ! "

But a poem like this occupies a special position among the dirges. As a rule these are addressed to Jahveh— they are in the proper sense " prayers," with the characteristic invocation to God in the second person, " O Jahveh, hear me." The third passage in this chapter, with which we shall deal later, opens with this style of address. But in the passage before us now Jahveh is spoken of throughout in the third person. It is therefore not a " prayer," but a " religious meditation." And there is a further difference between our passage and the other dirges. The latter consist usually of a lament over the present distress and a petition for deliverance. But here there is almost no lament. It is only hinted at in the parenthesis contained in verses 8b, 9a. Nor is there any express petition to Jahveh. It is evidently a quite special mood that finds voice here. There is no need to dwell on the distress that is being experienced. God knows it already. Nor is any special petition required. God hears the unspoken desire of the soul. It is something else that fills the speaker's heart. He desires to express his *confidence* in God's help, his hope in deliverance to come. It is this that relieves the sore heart, and God, hearing these confident words, cannot let this outstretched hand be drawn back empty. We have many poems of this kind—the so-called *Songs or Psalms of Trust*—containing thoughts of comfort such as occur in many of the dirges. Here they form the whole content of the poem.[1]

[1] Such Songs of Trust are Pss. iv ; xi ; xvi ; xxiii ; xxvii. 1–6 ; lxii ; cxxxi.

So far we have taken the poem as an Individual Dirge and interpreted it from that point of view. But it has other features which lead us to a quite unique conception of the whole Psalm. The "I" here speaks of an "enemy," but the word used for enemy is feminine. The authors of the Individual Dirges, often as they speak of enemies, never use such a word. They always refer to their persecutors as *men*. The speaker here must therefore also be a female. The punctuators of the text were conscious of this and vocalized the word as 'elohāyich. But we never find female speakers in the dirges of the Psalter. The two female disputants must therefore be understood allegorically, and, although there is no parallel to this in the Psalter, there are several parallels to it in the prophetical writings.

The prophets were so accustomed to personify Jerusalem and Zion that they occasionally went so far as to put words into their mouths.[1] To them, seeing the city in distress, it was natural to speak of her as mourning and to clothe her cry of lamentation in the dress of the dirge.[2] More rarely Israel and Judah are similarly personified.[3] The Hebrew poets and prophets thus carried over into the national religion forms of expression which had been originally used to express personal religious experience. No doubt personal poetry was richer and more impressive than the other (indeed, that is clear from the examples we still have), so that there was good reason why the authors of poems expres-

---

[1] Cf. Is. xlix. 21 ; Jer. xxii. 21 ; lvii. 35.
[2] Is. xl. 27 ; xlix. 14 ; Jer. iii. 4 f. ; iv. 31 ; x. 19–22 ; Pss. of Solomon i.; Baruch iv. 9–29 ; Lam. i. 9, 11–16, 18–22 ; ii. 20–22. An eschatological Hymn of Zion, Is. lxi. 10.
[3] Words of Israel, Jer. ii. 23, 25, 35. A Dirge of Ephraim, Jer. xxxi. 18 f. A Song of Praise of Israel, Ps. cxxix. An Eschatological Hymn of Israel, Is. xii. 1 f.

sive of national religion should borrow from it. Some modern expositors are fond of speaking in such cases of the "personified community," but the linguistic usage of the Old Testament lends no support to this interpretation. There is still less justification for using these passages to support the view that the " I " of the Psalms means "the community." This interpretation of the " I " is only permissible in some exceptional cases where it is clearly expressed or at least indicated by the external or internal connection of the passage.[1]

The closing lines of verse 10 in our passage indicate the actual political situation. The enemy will be "trampled like the dirt of the street." This is the very phrase that is used of peoples.[2] And the fact that this meaning is left unindicated in verse 7, and merely hinted at in the female "enemy" in verse 8, and expressly stated only in the last words of verse 10, is in entire keeping with the prophetical style, which was fond of disclosing a message in this gradual way.[3]

Applying the principles of literary history, we thus find that the poet is carrying over and applying to Zion *motifs* of the Individual Dirge. Where the dirge-writer speaks of his adversaries, our poet speaks of Zion's "female foe." She is not here blamed for Zion's misfortune, and therefore can neither be one of the world empires nor the whole heathen world, although this latter view is often taken. The poet means one of the small adjacent peoples who were exulting over Zion's misfortune—probably "the daughter of Edom,"

[1] Cf. E. Balla, *Ich der Psalmen*, p. 114 ff.
[2] Cf. Is. x. 6 ; xxviii. 18 ; 2 Sam. xxii. 43 = Ps. xviii. 42 ; Zech. x. 5.
[3] Cf. my Introductions to Schmidt, *Die Grossen Propheten*, 2nd ed., p. xlviii.

who showed special bitterness towards Zion [1] and exulted maliciously when Jerusalem fell.[2] The fate of Edom is contrasted with that of Zion in Lam. iv. 22, and Obadiah, verse 17 f., and Obadiah (verse 12 f.) cries to Edom, "Exult not over the children of Judah in the day of their destruction."

The theme of our passage is thus *Zion's confident hope*, and the accuracy of this political interpretation is confirmed by a number of details for which there are parallels both in the prophetic writings and in the national psalms. The poem opens with the conviction that Jahveh's anger lies heavy upon Zion, and that this anger is due to Zion's own sins. This conviction was deeply felt among the Jews when Jerusalem fell and long afterwards.[3] But the poem also expresses the conviction that the stranger's exultation will not last for ever, for many of the enemy's doings are not God's will.[4] The day is coming when Jahveh will maintain Zion's cause [5] and lead the people out of "darkness" into "light,"[6] and "justify"[7] it in the sight of the whole world. And when Zion's visitation has ended, Jahveh's wrath will be poured out against the evil doings of the heathen,[8] and those who said, "Where is Jahveh, your God?"[9] will be brought to shame and dishonour.[10]

[1] Is. xxxiv. 6; Ezek. xxxv. 5, 11; Ps. cxxxvii. 7.
[2] Ezek. xxxv. 14; Lam. iv. 22; Obad. xi.
[3] Is. xlii. 24 f.; Zech. i. 2.
[4] Is. x. 5 ff.; Hab. i. 11; Zech. i. 15.
[5] Is. xl. 27. Cf. Ps. ix. 5.
[6] For these metaphors cf. Amos v. 18; Is. ix. 1; xlii. 16.
[7] For this word used of Jahveh's action towards Israel cf. Ps. xcviii. 2.   [8] Is. xxvi. 20.
[9] Spoken by the heathen in Pss. lxxix. 10; cxv. 2; Joel ii. 17.
[10] Said of the heathen, Pss. lxxxiii. 17 f.; cxxix. 5; also Obadiah verse 10; Ezek. vii. 18.

THE CLOSE OF MICAH

This poem must have been sung on a day of humiliation, at one of the great fasts held in the sanctuary, in the presence of the assembled nation. Such celebrations were held from the earliest times in days of pestilence, danger from foreign enemies, famine, with all sorts of traditional ceremonies, and were regularly repeated from the fall of Jerusalem onwards.[1] The National Dirges contained in the Psalter were sung on such occasions,[2] and it must have been a specially impressive service when on such a day suffering Zion herself opened her lips in prayer to God.

2.

The second passage, Micah vii. 11-13, is, from the point of view of literary history, far simpler than the preceding poem, but modern expositors have found it all the more difficult to interpret. It reads:

11. The day for thy walls to be builded
    ' that ' day [3]—the time hastes on.[4]   3 + 3
12. That day, when ' they come ' ' to thee '[5]
    from Assyria   ' as far as '[6] Egypt   3 + 4
    and from ' Tyre '   to the river
    from sea to sea   and ' from ' mountain
                         to mountain.   4 + 4
13. But the earth becomes a desert
    because of its peoples, and the fruit of
    their deeds.   3 + 3

One glance is sufficient to enable anyone who has begun to notice such things to see that this passage

---

[1] Zech. iv.
[2] Cf. my *Einleitung in die Psalmen*, which is to appear immediately.
[3] For alterations of the text not otherwise discussed, see Kittel's *Biblia Hebraica*.
[4] Yidhag. For the meaning cf. Hab. ii. 3.
[5] We'adayich.   [6] Wa'adē.

belongs to a different literary "type." For one thing, Zion is no longer the speaker. She is being addressed. "Thy walls." "They come to thee." Further, the tone is quite different. Though, as in the preceding passage, a happy future is here spoken of, it is announced, predicted, whereas in the former passage it was yearningly desired. Another indication that we have passed to something different is the change of metre—till now it was mostly "fives," now it is "double threes," expanded once to a "seven" and once to an "eight." Long ago Ewald saw that this passage was a *prediction*, a *prophetic* oracle. The content is largely prophetic. There is the prophecy that Jerusalem's walls will one day be rebuilt [1] and the city become a centre for the whole world: her lost children shall return home from every quarter,[2] and all the heathen shall seek the dwelling-place of the most High,[3] while the whole earth shall become a desert.[4] There is also the prophetic addition that this glorious time is already imminent; this hope was uttered by the prophets for centuries. Prophetic, too, is the *mysterious tone* that is heard throughout the short passage. As Ewald said, the piece is full of half-expressed hints and incomplete words. A new speaker appears, but it is not plainly said who he is. A female is addressed, but who she is is left unsaid. We are only allowed to guess that Jahveh is speaking to Zion. This peculiar tone colours the whole passage:

> The day for thy walls to be builded,
> that day—the time hastes on.

---

[1] Is. lx. 10; Pss. li. 20; cii. 14 ff.; cxlvii. 2.
[2] Ezek. xxxiv. 13; Is. xi. 15; Micah ii. 12 f.; iv. 68 f.; Amos ix. 9; Zech. x. 8 ff.; Is. xxvii. 12; Pss. lxviii. 23; cvi. 47; cxlvii. 2.
[3] Is. ii. 2 f.; lx. 3 ff.; Zech. xiv. 16; Ps. cii. 23.
[4] Zech. xiv. 17.

It is a very impressive opening, as if this rebuilding had been already mentioned. And what "time" is meant? We may guess it means "the time appointed by Jahveh," but it is not said. Nor are we definitely told who is coming to Zion. The oracle leaves it indefinite: "they come." This obscurity, clearly intentional, is in the usual prophetic manner. The prophets received their revelations in mysterious hours of ecstasy and would have considered it unbecoming in them to desecrate God's secrets by exposing them to the full light of day.[1] But this tone of mystery is suffused with a note of exultation—it is a glorious future that awaits Zion. This exultant prediction of a coming day, glorious, but still wrapped in the veil of mystery—that is the language of the prophets of salvation, so familiar to us from the time of Deutero-Isaiah.[2] And then in the language of hyperbole the distant ends of the earth are named from which Zion's children shall return: "from Assyria as far as Egypt,"[3] "from Tyre to the river," and in a final burst of rapture, "from sea to sea, from mountain range to mountain range."[4]

The question now arises whether this prophetic passage has any connection at all with what precedes, or whether it is a separate independent poem. Sellin takes the latter view. But the question cannot be answered from the text alone. We must first inquire whether there is any other example of such a combination of National Dirge and Oracle. I have already tried to do this.[5] From numerous passages in the Old Testament we learn that it was customary to inquire of the oracle of

[1] See Hans Schmidt, *Die Grossen Propheten*, 2nd ed., p. xlvi ff.
[2] *Ibid.*, p. xlviii f.   [3] Zech. x. 10.
[4] Zech. ix. 10; Ps. lxxii. 8.
[5] Schmidt, *Die Grossen Propheten*, p. lviii ff., and *Einleitung in die Psalmen*, § 4, 14.

Jahveh on the occasion of a day of lamentation.[1] When Israel was defeated, Joshua wept and prayed before Jahveh and received his answer.[2] In Chronicles [3] we read that when war was in the air the king commanded a fast and offered in person the prayer, receiving in reply the promise of divine aid. Hezekiah's prayer was answered by the oracle through the mouth of Isaiah.[4] At the fast commanded by Jehoiachim, Jeremiah caused Baruch to read aloud the words of Jahveh.[5] Joel gives the dirge which the priests were to sing at the fast held on occasion of the plague of locusts,[6] and announces at the same time the gracious promises of God [7] given in reply. Habakkuk gives the nation's dirge at a time of distress and tells how he received in reply a message of comfort from Jahveh.[8] This seems to imply that it was the practice in Israel, when the dirge had been chanted, for the priest or prophet to lift up his voice and communicate the divine answer to the praying people. The same course was followed in Babylonia and Egypt. There the oracle comes immediately in response to the royal dirge.[9] The prophets adopted this popular custom and imitated those "liturgies," in which the National Dirge was followed by the divine voice promising deliverance. There are nearly a score of such combinations of National Dirge and Oracle.[10]

---

[1] Judges xx. 23, 26.   [2] Joshua vii. 7.   [3] 2 Chron. xx. 3 ff.
[4] Is. xxxvii. 14, 21.   [5] Jer. xxxvi.   [6] Joel ii. 17.
[7] Joel ii. 18.   [8] Hab. i. 12 ; ii. 1.
[9] Zimmern, *Babylonische Hymnen und Gebete*, p. 8, vol. ii, pp. 20 f. ; Erman, *Ägypten*, p. 525.
[10] Is. xxvi. 8–14a, 14b f. ; xxvi. 16–18, 19–21 ; xxxiii. 2, 3–6 ; xxxiii. 7–9, 10–12 ; xlix. 14, 15 ff. ; xlix. 24, 25 f. ; lix. 9–15a, 15b–20 ; lxiii. 7–lxiv. 11 ; lxv. ; Jer. iii. 22b–25 ; iv. 1 ; xiv. 2–9, 10 ; xiv. 19–22 ; xv. 1 ; xxxi. 18 f., 20 ; li. 34 f., 36 ff. ; Hosea vi. 1–3, 4–6 ; xiv. 3, 5–9 ; Hab. i. 2–4, 5 ff. ; i. 12–17 ; ii. 1. Cf. also Joel i. 5–ii. 11, with the oracle ii. 12–14 ; ii. 15–17 with the oracle ii. 18 ff., and Baruch iv. 9–29, 30 ff.

THE CLOSE OF MICAH

The absence of any express mention of a change of speaker explains why the interconnection has not been recognized.

One example may suffice here. When the enemy is at the gates, the National Dirge pleads:

> O Lord, be gracious to us. On Thee we wait.
> Be 'our' arm every morning
> and our help in the hour of need.

In reply, the divine oracle predicts the destruction of the enemy peoples:

> At the loud tumult the nations flee,
> at Thy anger the heathen are scattered.[1]

We have still to see whether there is any inherent connection between the dirge (verses 7-10) and the oracle (verses 11-13). For one thing, the theme of both is *Zion*. The dirge describes how Zion is on the lookout to see whether the night will soon be past and the day dawn when Jahveh will have mercy upon her; how she meantime bows humbly under the strokes of the divine rod, and does not lose heart even amid the scornful laughter of her foe. Such a Zion is surely prepared to hear the oracle confirming her faith, and to Zion thus prepared the message comes: Thou didst well to hope in Jahveh. According to thy faith, be it unto thee. Though thou art still desolate, a destroyed city without inhabitants, thou wilt arise as a fortress, a populous centre of the world. And upon thy foes, nay, upon the whole earth, will descend just judgment and destruction.

The two passages thus fit well together, and the whole is a well-arranged work of art. The impression made by the second passage with its divine confidence

[1] Is. xxxiii. 2 f.

is all the greater because it follows the first part with its human fears and longings. It is this alternation of moods that constitutes the beauty of these otherwise simple poems. By means of this "liturgical" form the poet is able to set forth not only one aspect of the religion of the people, but its whole content. In this inherent connection of the two passages we have a confirmation of our view that the "I" of the first passage is Zion.

3.

The third passage, verses 14–17, is as follows:

14. Guide Thy people with Thy staff,	
the sheep of Thine inheritance,	3 + 2
'which' 'dwell' so solitary in the scrub,	
in the midst of the garden.	3 + 2
15. Let them feed in Bashan and Gilead,	
as in days of old;	3 + 2
As of old, when thou cam'st out of 'I' Egypt	
'grant' us to see wonders.	3 + 2
16. Let the heathen see this and despair	
of all their might,	3 + 2
Lay their hand on their mouth,	
let their ears become deaf.	3 + 2
17. Let them eat dust like the serpents,	
like the things that crawl.	3 + 2
From their holes let them tremble 'IV'[1]	
and fear before Thee.	3 + 2

As in the first passage, the metre here is "double fives," i.e. the metre of the second passage is abandoned and that of the first is resumed. There is a similar

---

[1] 'Tremble before Jahveh, our God,' is the metre in its completed form. This is favoured by the sudden mention here of Jahveh in the third person.

THE CLOSE OF MICAH

connection between the contents of the two passages. After the lofty tone of the second passage, this third passage plunges again into the depths and opens with an earnest petition, " Guide Thy people with Thy staff," thus resembling the first passage, which also utters human hopes and desires.

The meaning becomes clearer when we again study the *type* to which the passage belongs. Jahveh is addressed in verse 14, i.e. that verse is a " prayer."[1] It is a " we " that speaks in verse 15. The " we " call themselves " Thy people," " the sheep of Thy inheritance," i.e. it is a prayer of *Israel*. It contains petitions, desires, and (expressed or tacit) laments, i.e. it is a " National Dirge." There are many of these in the Psalter.[2] They were sung at great services in days of national distress, and it must have been on some such occasion that this third passage was sung. We need not be surprised to find a National Dirge among the writings of a prophet. The prophets adopted this type on many occasions, thus making themselves the mouthpiece of their suffering nation.[3]

This helps us to understand the content of the passage. The prayer opens with the ardent petition, " Guide Thy people with Thy staff, the sheep of Thine inheritance." Such petitions were meant to touch Jahveh's heart, and therefore took a form which could not (it was hoped) fail to achieve their purpose. Jahveh is again and again reminded that His own cause is at stake, hence the words " Thy people," " the sheep of Thine inheritance." The same thing occurs in other Dirge psalms. " Thy

---

[1] Cf. my *Einleitung in die Psalmen*, § 4, 4.
[2] Cf. Pss. xliv, lxxiv, lxxix, lxxx, lxxxiii ; Lam. v.
[3] Is. lix. 9–15 ; lxiii. 11–lxiv. 11 ; Jer. iii. 22b–25 ; xiv. 2 9. 19–22 ; Hosea vi. 1–3 ; xiv. 3 f.

people "; [1] "Thy inheritance"; [2] "The tribe of Thine inheritance"; [3] "The sheep of Thy pasture." [4] Can Jahveh, God of Israel, forget His own people? Can the Shepherd of Israel (Ps. lxxx. 1) forget His own flock? A specially effective turn is given in the phrase "with His (own) staff," expressing the tacit contrast that at the moment Jahveh's flock is being badly guided by alien shepherds. In another prophetical dirge [5] we read, "Jahveh, other lords beside Thee have dominion over us." The words that follow, "which dwell solitary in the scrub, in the midst of the garden" (verse 14b), contain a brief lament inserted between the petitions and desires. They depict the sad state of Jahveh's flock under the guidance of the wicked shepherds: the sheep are compelled to seek their scanty food alone in the scrub, in the "desert," while all around them is the fair "garden" which they are not allowed to enter. The same contrast between "desert" and "garden" is found elsewhere.[6] The object in view is to enlist Jahveh's compassion. The meaning is, it is faring badly with the Jews under foreign dominion in their desolate, untilled land. Then follows verse 14c, a *desire*, in continuance of the petition. Such "desires," of which we had an example in verse 10, and shall have another in verses 16 f., differ from the "prayer" proper, being couched not in the Imperative, but in the Jussive.[7] "May they pasture in Bashan and Gilead, as in the days of yore." It was with sadness that the Jews thought of the fair lands which their nation had once

---

[1] Pss. lxxxiii. 4; xciv. 5.　　　[2] Pss. lxxix. 1; xciv. 5.
[3] Ps. lxxiv. 2.
[4] Ps. lxxiv. 1. Cf. my *Einleitung in die Psalmen*, § 4, 9
[5] Isa. xxvi. 13.
[6] Is. xxix. 17; xxxii. 15.
[7] Cf. my *Einleitung in die Psalmen*, § 4, 8.

possessed. Bashan and Gilead are mentioned here [1] because of the metaphor that has just been employed. They afford splendid *pasture*. And another thought emerges at this point. The prophets had taken it for granted that the ancient conditions would return. That was a conception on which they loved to dwell. Hence the hope of Israel that their first redemption from Egypt would be followed by a second, a similar redemption. Hence the desire in this passage that Bashan and Gilead, which had once been theirs, should again be their pasture. This leads up to the further petition of verse 15, that once again the wonders might be repeated which God had of old accomplished by the hand of Moses. " Show new signs and repeat the wonders." [2] The National Dirges delighted to recall the glorious days of the past, when Jahveh's aid was freely given—in particular the exodus from Egypt and the conquest of Canaan.[3] Such mention may have originally been a sort of " analogy-magic "—the mention of the ancient events was meant to awaken the old power. In our texts it has the higher purpose of reminding God of His own might and giving confidence to the suppliants. In verse 16 the climax is reached. The " desire " gains in intensity : " Let the heathen see this and despair of all their might." In the National Dirges the petition frequently leads up to the thought that the hearing of the prayer might cause the world to know God's greatness and all the heathen be ashamed. " Lift up Thy hand against the strange nations, that they may see Thy mighty power. That they may know Thee, as we have known Thee, that there is no God beside Thee." [4]

---

[1] Zech. x. 10 ; Jer. l. 19.   [2] Ecclus. xxxvi. 6.
[3] Pss. xliv. 2–4 ; lxxiv. 2 ; lxxx. 9–12 ; Is. lxiii. 11–14.
[4] Ecclus. xxxvi. 3, 5.

138 WHAT REMAINS OF THE OLD TESTAMENT

> Let them be ashamed and dismayed for ever,
> Let them be confounded and perish.
> That (in especial) they may know that Thou, ' I,' Jahveh, alone
> Art the Most High over all the earth. [1]

And again:

> Hearken to the prayer of Thy servants,
> According to Thy grace toward Thy people,
> That the ends of the earth may know,
> That Thou art the everlasting God. [2]

Then comes a rush of ardent desires in verses 16 and 17: that the enemy in their terror may lose the power both to speak and to hear, and, as a sign that they will keep silence, lay their hand upon their mouth; [3] that the thunder of the divine manifestation [4] may render them deaf. It was customary for the vanquished to kiss the victor's feet. At the Egyptian Court it was an exceptional mark of the royal grace when the king allowed one of his nobles to kiss his feet instead of the ground on which his feet rested.[5] That is the meaning of the desire expressed here that the heathen should kiss the dust, or rather, with the passionate hyperbole so characteristic of Hebrew poetry, that they should *eat* the dust, like serpents.[6] Nor is this all. After the prophetical manner, the poet visualizes the final condition. The heathen lords, at present dominating God's people, shall then be vanquished and taken captive and tremble before Jahveh's judgments. There is a similar expression at the close of one of the royal psalms in which a world conquest is described.[7]

---

[1] Ps. lxxxiii. 18 f.
[2] Ecclus. xxxvi. 17.
[3] Job xxi. 5; xxix. 9; xl. 4; Judges xviii. 19. Cf. Is. lii. 15.
[4] Is. xxxiii. 3.
[5] Erman, *Ägypten*, p. 109.
[6] Is. xlix. 23; Ps. lxxii 9; Gen. iii. 14.
[7] Ps. xviii. 46.

THE CLOSE OF MICAH

Our estimate of this third passage is therefore as follows: It is a National Dirge, but it is suffused with the prophetical spirit. The deliverance which is here desired is the fulfilment of the promises announced by the prophets. The only difference between it and the ordinary dirge is the absence of the invariable invocation of Jahveh in the vocative case. And so, as over the first passage, there broods over this otherwise clear poem some of the mysteriousness so characteristic of the prophetical writings.

4.

The fourth and last extract is contained in verses 18 to 20.

18. Who is a God like 'Him'[1]	that forgiveth sin,	
and pardoneth the guilt	of the remnant of His heritage?	$4 + 4$
He retaineth not His anger for ever,		
but delighteth in mercy.		$3 + 3$
19. He will have mercy upon us again,		
and 'wash away' our sins;[2]		$2 + 2$
'will'[3] cast into the depths of the sea		
all 'our' iniquities.		$3 + 2$
20. To Jacob Thou wilt show truth		
and to Abraham grace,		$3 + 2$
As[4] Thou to our fathers didst swear		
in the days of old.		$3 + 2$

The two closing strophes consist of "fives" with one admixture (19a) of a "four." The first strophe (verse 18) stands apart from these, and begins strongly with an "eight" and ends with the calmer "double threes."

---

[1] In verses 18 and 19a there is a change of person. See below.
[2] Y^{e}kabbēs. [3] W^{e}yashlich. [4] Ka'^{a}sher.

There is not only a mixture of metre, but also a mixture of type in this passage. With regard to verse 18 there is no uncertainty. It is a *Rhetorical Question*, and this is a characteristic feature of the *Hymn*. A few typical examples may be quoted. "Who is like unto the Lord, our God?"[1] "Who is God, save Jahveh? and who is a rock beside our God?"[2] "Who is a great God like our God?"[3] "Who in the skies is like the Lord?"[4] There are nearly fifty such Rhetorical Questions in the Hymns of the Old Testament, and they are also frequent in Babylonian hymns.[5] There is also another rarer form, "*No one* is holy like Jahveh, there is no rock like our God."[6] The Question occurs usually in the third and second person. "Who is like *Him*?" or "Who is like *Thee*?" In our text there is some confusion. The third person is correct here, as in verses 18*b* and 19*a*. The question is usually followed by participial constructions, which appear in our translation as relative clauses. "Who is a God like Him, who forgiveth sins?" The same construction is found in Ps. xviii. 31–34. In the Hebrew these are participles.[7] These are followed either by relative clauses [8] or by principal clauses [9] which enlarge on the uniqueness of Jahveh. Here we have principal clauses, verses 18*b* and 19. In the last strophe the third person is replaced by the second. Both occur in the Hymns, and the same change is found in the Psalms.[10] In content also

---

[1] Ps. cxiii. 5. [2] Ps. xviii. 31.
[3] Ps. lxxvii. 14; Job xxxvi. 22. [4] Ps. lxxxix. 6.
[5] Stummer, *Sumerischakkadische Parallelen*, p. 57.
[6] 1 Sam. ii. 2.
[7] Pss. xxxv. 10; lxxxix. 8; cxii. 5 ff.; Exod. xv. 11; Deut. xxxiii. 26; 1 Kings viii. 23.
[8] 1 Kings viii. 24. [9] Ps. xviii. 36, Exod. xv. 12.
[10] *Einleitung in die Psalmen*, § 2, 24.

THE CLOSE OF MICAH

the last strophe resembles the Hymns. It declares the uniqueness of Jahveh, and contains such words as "He will not keep His anger for ever" and "He takes pleasure in mercy."[1] Altogether, in content and language, it belongs to the Hymn type.

The Hymn, of which there are very numerous examples in the Old Testament, was originally sung at the great festivals. Its characteristic note is enthusiasm and reverence towards God's Majesty. Because of its popularity, it had a strong influence on other types of poetry.[2]

This fourth passage is therefore a new type and it strikes a new note. The previous passages were laden with petitions and desires. Here we have whole-hearted exultation and rejoicing. This change is emphasized by the new metre and by the change of person. The former passages were addressed to Jahveh; this speaks of Him, and it is only at the very end, in verse 20, that the more intimate tone is resumed. The connection of thought with what precedes is also clear. What the nation has been praying for has now become a certainty, and the people now with joy declare their *faith* in the future: "He will have mercy upon us again and wash away our sins" (verse 19). "Thou wilt remember the fathers in the persons of their children and not forget Thine oath" (verse 20). This appeal to the promises and the fathers is frequent in the National Dirges,[3] and there are many parallels to such a closing note. After all the wrestlings in prayer, certainty fills the hearts of the people, and they rise to the faith that "*He will* tread down our enemies";[4] "*Thou wilt* have mercy

[1] Pss. ciii. 9; xxxiii. 5.   [2] *Einleitung in die Psalmen*, § 2.
[3] Ps. lxxxix. 50; Jer. xiv. 21; Ecclus. xxxvi. 20.
[4] Ps. lx. 14.

on Jacob for ever; *Thou wilt* raise us up in the day of Thy help";[1] "Thine ear *will* hear the sigh of their heart."[2] The Hymn type is therefore a fitting close. "We will give Thee thanks for ever and show forth Thy praise to all generations."[3] The Individual Dirges supply many parallel passages in which this expression of confidence that prayer will be heard is followed by a Song of Praise or Hymn.[4] We can compare the Hymn in verse 18 with the "eschatological hymns" which prophets like Deutero-Isaiah sung to declare their assurance of coming deliverance.[5]

5.

Let us now sum up our results. The four passages examined fall into two pairs:

A { I. A *Dirge of Zion*, answered by
    II. A *Divine Oracle*.
B { III. A *Dirge of Israel*, continued by
    IV. A *Hymn* of assurance of future deliverance.

The question arises whether A and B are in merely fortuitous juxtaposition in this chapter, or whether they form an intentional comprehensive unity.

Let us once more begin by asking whether the Old Testament contains any other examples of compositions which thus cover the same ground twice. As a matter of fact, this was a favourite method in Hebrew poetry. In Psalm xxiv the temple choristers twice address the sacred gates and call forth a reply on each occasion.

---

[1] Psalms of Solomon, vii. 8, 10. [2] Ps. x. 17.
[3] Ps. lxxix. 13.
[4] *Einleitung in die Psalmen*, § 2, 56. [5] *Ibid.*, § 51.

THE CLOSE OF MICAH

There are many Hymns which twice reach a climax, on each occasion following upon an invocation,[1] and there are even cases where such climax is threefold.[2] In Psalm xviii we have a royal Song of Praise with a double account of deliverance and a double ascription of thanksgiving,[3] and Ps. cxvi. 1 ff., 10 ff., is an example of an Individual Song of Praise containing a double account of affliction, deliverance, and thanksgiving. In particular the Individual Dirges exhibit this double recapitulation of the whole progression through plaint and petition to confidence and praise,[4] and in two other cases a recurrent refrain gives memorable emphasis to a triple flow and ebb of the same religious emotions.[5] In Psalm xciv, which contains *motifs* both of National and Individual Dirge, the first part ends in verse 15 at a climax of confidence, and the second part begins again in verse 16 with yearning and plaint. For our purpose it is specially interesting to find that the authors of such "liturgies" were fond of combining Dirge and Oracle. In a Babylonian hymn the prayer of King Assurbanipal and the favourable answer of the deity are repeated three times.[6] In Psalm cxxi, a dialogue between a suppliant and the priest, verse 1 and verse 3 give a double consolation to doubting question and timid desire.[7] In Is. xxxiii. 2, 3-6, a brief dirge is answered by a more lengthy oracle, but in verses 7-9

[1] Pss. xcv. 1 ff., 6 f.; xcvi. 1 ff., 7 ff.; xcviii. 1 ff., 8 ff.; c. 1 ff., 4 ff.; cxlviii. 1 ff., 7 ff.; cxlix. 1 ff., 5 ff.

[2] Pss. lxvi. 1, 5, 8; cxlv. 1, 4, 10; cxlvii. 1, 7, 12.

[3] Ps. xviii. 2 ff., 32 ff.

[4] Pss. xxxi. 2 ff., 10 ff.; xxxv. 1 ff., 11 ff.; lxxxvi. 1 ff., 14 ff.; cii. 2 ff., 24 ff.

[5] Pss. xlii and xliii; lxxi. 1, 9, 17.

[6] Zimmern, *Babylonische Hymnen und Gebete*, II. Auswahl, p. 20 f.

[7] See the exposition in my *Commentary on the Psalms*.

the dirge is resumed, to be finally silenced by a mighty word of Jahveh in verses 10 ff. Thus the arrangement which we have here, giving four passages, the first being akin to the third and the second to the fourth, while the main section arises from the second, is very common in Hebrew poetry. This practice of duplication was adopted from the temple service, where it was meant to reinforce the power of the sacred word, and was used as a means of giving emphasis to what was considered important.[1] Later religious writers borrowed it in order to produce their effects. Naturally they aimed at varying the first part and at the same time transcending it in the second part. Cf. Is. xxxiii and Ps. cxvi.

We are now in a position to see whether the close of Micah is not an artistic composition of this kind, and whether the details of the separate sections are such as to make the whole passage a unity. Let us first try to reconstruct the *historical position* implied.

Zion and its citizens are living under intolerable conditions. The city is sparsely inhabited and has no walls (verse 11); the land is poorly tilled—a wilderness, and foreign shepherds oppress the people (verse 14). The fall of the city long ago is still a painful memory (verse 8). Israel is now only a "remnant" from a better past (verse 18). The Jews are scattered over the whole world, "from Assyria to Egypt and from Tyre to the river" (verse 12), and everywhere they are at enmity with the peoples among whom they live. They complain of the malice of "the inhabitants of the world" (verse 13). It cannot be hidden or gainsaid—

---

[1] There is a similar connection between Is. xxvi. 8–14*a*, 14*b*, 15; 16–18, 19–21; Habakkuk i. 2–4, 5–11; i. 12–17, ii. 1 ff.; Joel i. 5–ii. 11, 12–14; ii. 15–17, 18–27.

THE CLOSE OF MICAH

Jahveh's anger still rests upon His inheritance (verse 9). Zion has been brought low and "sits in darkness" (verse 8), and the wicked enemy, the daughter of Edom, has every reason for her malicious exultation (verse 8). All this gives a consistent, coherent picture of Zion's condition.

But *Zion's faith* still lives, that faith which the prophets preached and did so much to maintain. Jahveh cannot keep His anger for ever, for He is a God that delighteth in mercy (verse 18). He will not always turn a deaf ear to Zion's prayers and her brokenness of spirit, nor continue to overlook her devoted, faithful waiting (verse 8). Above all, He cannot forget the mercy and truth which He solemnly swore to Jacob and Abraham (verse 20). The righteous God will not allow the wickedness of the whole world to go unjudged (verse 13). The God Who demands uprightness cannot permit His holy name to be spoken against wickedly (verse 10). He Who guards His people will surely come to guide them with His own staff (verse 14). He must acknowledge that Zion, grievously as she has sinned against Him, is not in the wrong as against the heathen, and He will one day take up the just cause of the oppressed (verse 9). These numerous motives for action on the part of Jahveh are all in harmony with each other and prove how zealous the Hebrews were in finding sure bases for their faith. They are all summed up in the first sentence—Zion awaits confidently a new day and is looking out to see whether there are yet no signs of its coming (verse 7).

Then there is the *picture of the future* that beckons to this faith. By and by there will come a great change for Zion and for the whole world. Jahveh will appear, and before Him all the empires of the world shall be abased (verse 16). The heathen, once the proud rulers of the world, will lick the dust at His feet, and from the prisons into which they have been thrown they will await in dread the judgment that will be passed upon them (verse 17). The whole earth where they dwell will become a desert (verse 13). Thus the arrogance of the heathen will be brought low (verse 16) and their wickedness avenged (verse 13). In particular, proud Edom will be brought to shame and trodden like the dirt of the street (verse 10). While this dreadful fate overtakes the heathen world, Israel will be delivered and Zion will be transfigured. The wonders of the Exodus will be repeated (verse 15). The walls of Zion shall rise in their ancient glory and Zion shall be a place of pilgrimage for both Jews and heathen (verse 12). Jahveh in person will be their shepherd and lead them to pasture in long lost, but now regained, regions of Bashan and Gilead (verse 14). All His wrath is forgotten (verse 18); all their sins have been cast into the depths of the sea (verse 19). And, best of all, the day for all this is now near; it is hastening on (verse 11). It is clear that this picture of Israel's faith and hope is also a unity.

The poem should probably be dated about the time of Trito-Isaiah.[1] There is nothing to support the opinion [2] that it belongs to the Maccabean period.

Our last question is whether the two main groups A and B, with their different utterance of religious moods and thoughts, form an artistic whole. If so, the group B must both modify and transcend group A.[3] Now, speaking generally, the third passage merely

[1] Giesebrecht, *Beiträge zur Iesaiakritik*, p. 217.
[2] Marti, Paul Haupt, Nowack
[3] See *supra*, p. 142.

repeats the *motifs* of the first; both are Dirges, but there *is* a new element, viz. greater clearness of language. In the third passage Zion appears in a somewhat obscure personification; in the first, the nation speaks in the first person. In the third, the prayer is more passionate; while the first, more quietly and calmly, speaks of Jahveh only in the third person. Further, the contents are more comprehensive. In the first passage it is only Edom against whom vengeance is desired; in the third, the whole world is laid under the ban. There is a similar relationship between the second and fourth parts. While they are clearly different in form, a divine utterance in the former and a human outpouring in the other, they resemble each other in content. They both proclaim the certainty that deliverance is coming. In this case also the later passage transcends the former. In the former the community receives an oracle and raises a hymn of exultant confidence in the future. While the oracle is brief and obscure, the closing passage is full and clear. There are other "liturgies" and mixed poems which provide examples of the practice of concluding with a Hymn,[1] just as many of our cantatas close majestically with a resounding Hallelujah.

We have, therefore, in this close of Micah an artistically constructed unit. The poem was rendered as a "liturgy" by different singers on one of the "days of dule" in Jerusalem.

It is only when we are able to imagine it thus rendered that we can realize its power and depth. Of course, we can even then do so very imperfectly, for the music of ancient Israel is for us irrevocably lost. Still, we can picture to ourselves the passage A being sung as two

[1] Pss. xi. 7–9; cxv. 16–18; cxviii. 28; Deut. xxxiii. 26–29.

solos by two trained choristers, while B was rendered by the choir. That such solos were performed in the temple service can be inferred from the introductions to the Hymns, and the Hymns also prove that special effects were produced by the antiphonal renderings of soloists and choir.[1] There is little doubt also that an attempt was made to express the particular nature of the piece. In deep notes of restrained passionateness the pain and yearning of Zion was sung, and in response the mysterious and solemn voice of God became audible in words of consolation and cheer. The longing of human hearts was again expressed as the choir sang with fervour the prayers and desires of the people, and finally all sense of sorrow was lost in the hymn of exultation. It is only in this way that we can understand what poems like these meant for Jewish hearts—how their tears flowed as the dirge was sung, and how faith recovered strength when it heard the message of deliverance.

Long ago Ewald saw the relationship of the four passages we have studied, but modern expositors seem to have overlooked his exposition. In their ignorance of this organic method of exposition, they have applied all kinds of mechanical methods. They saw that our text does not at first sight read like one unit, and they concluded that the parts do not belong together. Objections were based on the presence of different metres, on the fact that there are several speakers and several persons who are addressed, and on the variety of the thoughts expressed, so they suggested deletions and alterations in order to get at the meaning of the chapter. In spite of all their endeavours, they failed to bring out the unity of the whole poem and fell back

[1] *Einleitung in die Psalmen*, § 2, 44.

on the suggestion that two or three separate poems have been accidentally brought together. We hope we have shown that our method points a way towards finding in the entire passage one comprehensive unit. The study may prove useful in connection with other similar investigations.

V

JACOB[1]

1.

THERE is still great divergence of opinion amongst scholars regarding the source and the original meaning of the patriarchal figures in the Bible. For a long time the discussion of this, the most important of all the questions raised by the latter part of Genesis, seemed to hang fire. The lengthy task of separating the documentary sources of this book pushed into the background all the other problems connected with Genesis. Of course this separation of the sources had to be carried through, or at least surveyed, before the deeper-lying questions could be taken in hand with any prospect of success. It is therefore, perhaps, not surprising that, although the original meaning of the patriarchal figures has in recent years been the subject of detailed discussion, no one view has yet been generally accepted as satisfactory.

Although the view contained in the tradition itself—that the patriarchs were really and literally historical persons—has by no means been universally surrendered, it is not now held with the same sure confidence as before. There can be no doubt whatever that the narratives which deal with the patriarchs are legends and not strict history; and if many scholars are still reluctant to give up the figure of Abraham, surely the historicity of Jacob cannot rouse anyone to enthusiasm.

[1] *Preussische Jahrbücher*, Band 176, Juni-Heft, 1919.

For what is there that should be historical about him? That on one occasion he deceived his blind father? Or that he fought hand to hand with a god? Or is it his journeys? This essay is intended to show that these do not belong to the original elements of the legend.

But if these patriarchal figures are not historical, what is it proposed to make of them? One scientific view, widely held for some time, was inclined to explain them as "degraded deities." It was at the time an accepted principle that legends had their origin in myths, and search was made in these narratives for mythical features. Winkler and the so-called "Pan-Babylonian School" claimed to have found such features. It is not overbold to say that this claim cannot be maintained. In the patriarchal narratives there are very few echoes of myth, perhaps none at all. In connection with Jacob there is no trace whatever of his ever having been a god or an heroic figure. Even his contest with a demon is no indication of this, for similar tales are frequent in folk-lore; nor is there any indication of it in the fact that the locality of his grave is mentioned, for he must be buried somewhere according to tradition. Nor is there any basis for the suggestion that he was a giant, and the statement that along with Laban he piled up a mountain as a boundary rampart is derived from later expositors, and does not belong to the original source.

There seemed to be a better scientific basis for another view, according to which the narratives are to be understood as describing events in the life of nations. This view, which prevailed for a long time among Wellhausen's followers, can claim some support in the ancient narratives, for, as is well known, these look upon the patriarchs in general as the ancestors of Israel. Jacob is identified with Israel, and his brother Esau is Israel's neighbour Edom; Laban is called the Aramæan, and in the legend he concludes a treaty with Jacob, which was understood to apply to the two peoples Israel and Aram. And it is plain that the deception of Esau by Jacob is meant to represent the retrogression of Edom before the younger people Israel. Further, the twelve sons of Jacob bear the names of the twelve tribes of Israel. And although some of the patriarchs bear names unknown to the documented history of Israel, it still seems legitimate to suppose that these refer to older prehistoric peoples and tribes, whose history found an echo in these legends and can still be reconstructed from them with the use of a little skill.

Now it cannot be disputed that there is some justification for this view. These stories contain elements which must be understood in that way. When twelve sons are ascribed to Jacob, that really means only that the people of Israel was made up of twelve tribes, just as the sons of Judah are simply the clans of the tribe of Judah. We shall meet with other examples of the same kind of interpretation. It must, however, have been very natural for the ancient Hebrew mind to conceive peoples and tribes as persons, and to interpret their history and their relations under the form of such events as take place between individuals. Still, the question remains whether the *whole* patriarchal history can be thus explained, and whether, therefore, Jacob can be explained as the name of a prehistoric tribe. We must also keep in mind the possibility that these legends contain, along with the history of peoples, some material of an entirely different kind, which is to us

JACOB

completely unintelligible. Fundamental questions of this kind could only be answered by experiment, i.e. some daring scholar had, at the risk of mistake, to endeavour to apply the principle to the whole of the material. To Steuernagel [1] belongs the credit of having made the attempt to explain the entire Jacob story in this ethnological way, but the results he obtained turned out so amazing that everyone could see the impossibility of giving this ethnological interpretation to the entire material. Take, e.g., Jacob's contest with the demon at Peniel—a narrative which has many parallels in similar stories and which can only be understood in connection with them. Steuernagel takes this to mean the victorious fight of the tribe Jacob with the inhabitants of the Peniel district. Joseph's coat of many colours, which aroused the envy of his brethren, Steuernagel interprets as meaning the superior dress of rich descendants of Joseph, which embittered against them the rest of the tribes of Israel! That is a kind of interpretation which has its ultimate roots in rationalism and which is nowadays obsolete. Ed. Meyer [2] rightly utters a warning against such exaggerations of an idea which, within proper limits, is true and fruitful. The result, therefore, is that, although part of the material must be understood ethnologically, only a part can be so understood, and in the following pages we hope to show that this part is not the most original constituent of the story. In any case we have as little proof of the existence of a people Jacob as we have for that of a people Laban, and we have no right to assume the existence of either.

If, then, figures like that of Jacob are neither historical

[1] Steuernagel, *Einwanderung der Israelitischen Stämme*, 1901.
[2] Ed. Meyer, *Die Israeliten und ihre Nachbarstämme*, p. 250.

figures nor gods of former days nor prehistoric tribes, what are they? The way to the answer has been indicated by Hugo Gressmann [1] in an essay which is, or at least in the present writer's opinion should have been, epoch-making in the history of Old Testament scholarship. He has suggested that these figures were originally the heroes of primitive narratives, i.e. so-called folk-tales, heroes who were only subsequently raised in Israel to the dignity of national ancestors. This assumes the accuracy of the opinion, which has recently come to the front and which has the support of W. Wundt, that the oldest narratives of humanity were not myths about the gods, but folk-tales, narratives which in a later and more developed age were combined with historical reminiscences and have thus become *sagas*.[2] Following up this view, Gressmann suggests that the patriarchal stories likewise contained an abundance of originally mythical material, and that even the ancestral figures themselves are to be understood in this way. It is this hypothesis that is to be thoroughly tested in the following pages, so far as concerns the figure of Jacob.[3]

---

[1] *Zeitschrift für die alttestamentliche Wissenschaft*, xxx, 1910, p. 1.

[2] Cf. my *Rel. geschl. Volksbuch. Märchen im A.T.*, 1917.

[3] Other studies preliminary to the present essay are as follows: I have dealt with the building up of the Jacob stories, taking the Esau narratives as the kernel of the whole, in my *Commentary on Genesis*, 1901, pp. 266 ff., and have attempted the separation of the historical material from the material of another kind, following Ed. Mayer, in the third edition of the same commentary, 1910. Then I gradually felt the force of Gressmann's hypothesis. Thus the complete idea of the Jacob stories has come to me from several sources. I have discussed it more briefly in the Encyclopedia, *Religion in Geschichte und Gegenwart*, article "Jacob and Esau." I have also tested in the same way the Joseph stories in *Zeitschrift der deutsch. morgenl. Gesellschaft*, 1922, vol. 76, pp. 55 ff.

2.

We have to traverse a long road in order to gain clearness in this matter, and the reason why the whole question has been treated so rarely with success is the fact that this road has not been followed with sufficient consistency. *We must analyse the entire literary composition which is attached to the name of Jacob, and try to discover its oldest component parts.*

Such an analysis must, of course, assume that the criticism of the sources—the narratives have come down to us in the combined recensions of J, E, and P—has been to some extent carried out. This is not altogether the case. Whole generations of scholars have been busied with this task. It was Wellhausen who taught us the nature of the latest source, P, and determined its age. Our purpose is not greatly affected by the separation of P. This writer has touched the Jacob stories but slightly. In our present text they play a very important part, but the older sources, J and E, were very much alike in these stories, and the detailed separation of these two must remain doubtful. Nor has the question, recently raised, been settled whether in the Jacob stories in J there are two threads to be disentangled.[1]

---

[1] Eissfeldt, in his *Hexateuch-Synopse*, 1922, distinguishes even a fourth source, the so-called Laienquelle. Thus, unfortunately, the criticism of the sources of Genesis resembles, not a well-founded and finely crowned edifice, but, in spite of, or perhaps just because of, all the pains that have been spent upon it, a web of Penelope, on which labour is ever recommenced anew. However disconcerting this may seem, it is not an insuperable obstacle to the study of our question. For all the sources which scholars have found, or imagined they have found, are in substantial agreement as far as the composition of the Jacob narrative is concerned. In all of them the figure of Jacob is essentially one and the same. (This is

When we now raise the question how this cycle of stories arose and how it is to be regarded, we enter upon a region of tradition that is *anterior to our sources*. Probably the individual Jacob stories existed in oral tradition many centuries previous to J and E, until, first in oral, then in written form, they were combined in the composite form in which we now have them.

This involves exactly the same presupposition as is made for the Gospel narratives, and indeed for all narratives that have come down to us by way of tradition, viz. that, as a rule, in oral tradition *each story existed by itself* as a separate entity. Needless to say, in Israel as elsewhere, each narrative was current separately, entirely unconnected with others, just as is the case still with our folk-tales and legends.[1] That this is also the case with the Jacob stories is proved by the fact that the figure of the patriarch differs greatly in the different narratives. In his relations with Esau and Laban he is the skilful shepherd; in the Peniel story he is the strong, fearless foeman; in the Joseph story he is the aged father with a special love for his youngest son. All combinations of individual stories into larger composites invariably belong to a relatively later stage.

Accordingly, in our analysis of the Jacob traditions, we must pay heed to the following points: First, we have to study each individual story by itself and determine its origin. In particular, we have to notice how

scarcely true for Eissfeldt's suggested Laienquelle.) The Source references here given (not very important in this connection) are taken from third, fourth, and fifth editions of my *Genesis Commentary*.

[1] To my great astonishment I see that there are Old Testament scholars unwilling to admit this quite self-evident statement, and who maintain that it is an unjustifiable dismemberment on my part of the sources. I can only attribute such an attitude to a complete lack of acquaintance with the study of folk-tales and legends.

JACOB

the historical element in it is interwoven with matter of another kind, probably taken from folk-tale, and to ask how this affects the figure of Jacob. Further, we have to determine in what order the individual stories came together into the composite whole. This can be learned from the closer or more remote relation which they bear to the whole. Such an investigation requires, of course, a certain *flair* or artistic sense, for which many scholars show an unconcealed dislike whenever it intrudes into scientific investigation. Unfortunately, however, the legends of Genesis are undeniably artistic productions, and, however strongly this claim may be resented, they cannot be understood without a feeling for their peculiar beauty. But, for the comfort of those who are suspicious of all æsthetic judgments, we may say at once that this essay will only involve very simple features of this kind which are easily intelligible to everyone. The reason why we are able to gather from the form of the composite narrative the manner in which the stories were gradually combined is that neither J nor E undertook to make a completely new work, but, in spite of all combinations and alterations and omissions and additions, they left on the whole the arrangement of the material in the form in which their predecessors had built it. This will be shown by detailed examples. Israel produced no Homer, so we are in a position—and this is specially true of the Jacob stories—to distinguish the later parts of the narratives from the earlier. The former are very easily recognizable from the looser relation in which they stand to the others.

By interpolating this investigation into the origin of the composite narrative between the criticism of the sources and the question as to the meaning of the patriarchal figures, we obtain a firmer foundation for our study of this latter question. We shall not, as has been done hitherto, capriciously take any narrative as the real Jacob narrative; we shall take that which is shown by the composite narrative itself to be the kernel of the whole.

It will be best to begin with the stories added at a later time, gradually separate these out, and thus reach the original core. To borrow a metaphor from geology, we shall first remove the upper layers in order to expose those beneath. Here we must distinguish *four groups* of stories, which we may compare to so many layers of soil. In chronological order these are:

I. Narratives about Jacob and Esau.

II. Narratives about Jacob and Laban.

The material in these two has been worked up into one cycle of stories. At the close of the first set Jacob flees to Laban, and at the end of his adventures there he returns to Esau, and then a second part of the Esau stories is narrated.

III. Narratives of theophanies and holy places. These are connected with definite localities and have been inserted into the already existing cycle at those points in the narrative where Jacob has reached the locality specified. They include the stories about Bethel, Peniel, Mahanaim, and Shechem.

IV. Stories about the children of Jacob, their birth and later fates, including those about Reuben, Simeon, Levi, Judah, and Joseph.

3.

Following the plan proposed, we begin with these latter stories. A glance at the style of the composite narrative shows that these were the last to be inserted into the cycle of Jacob stories ; but no conclusion is to be drawn from this as to their age as separate stories. In them Jacob plays only a subordinate part. He is the father of the actors in these stories. But the names of the chief figures are those of the *tribes of Israel*—that is to say, we have here *tribal legends*. The name of Jacob has come into these stories merely because he was regarded as the father of the tribal ancestors. As far as the figure of Jacob is concerned, therefore, all we learn from these is that at a certain time he was regarded as ancestor of the twelve tribes of Israel, just as in J he bears the byname "Israel." For our purpose we might omit these tribal legends altogether, and we linger over them a moment only because we intend to use them afterwards to throw light upon the Jacob stories proper.

There is the legend about Reuben (Gen. xxxv. 21 f.), given in one brief hint, which we have to supplement. It tells us that Reuben, Jacob's first-born son, has had relations with Jacob's concubine, Bilha, and has thereby drawn down upon himself his father's curse. As has already been said, in order to understand how such a narrative originated, we must carefully disentangle the various components out of which it has been formed. First of all, from other sources we are justified in assuming that the tribe of Reuben, which in the earliest period held the leading place among the tribes, had at a later time fallen into complete decay. This fall from its high estate is explained after the ancient fashion by the declaration that Reuben, the first-born among the brethren, had been cursed by the national ancestor. Thus far we have historical tradition in an antique poetic dress. Then the narrative was further developed by transferring to Reuben the popular *motif* with which we are familiar elsewhere,[1] viz. an adult son seduces his father's concubine and is expelled from the family. The historical element in this, therefore, is the tradition of Reuben's fall, whereas the actual content of the narrative is derived from the storehouse of poetical invention.

The case is similar with the *narrative about Judah* (Gen. xxxviii). Here also the basis of the story consists of reminiscences from the early history of the tribe. In the earliest period Judah contained three clans—Er, Onan, and Shela, of whom the first two perished early and two new ones, Perez and Serah, were formed. This was put into legendary dress by saying that Er and Onan died early, while Perez and Serah were posthumously born. Then we are told that the two who died early had one wife, Tamar, who in her widowhood succeeded in acquiring legitimate posterity, viz. Perez and Serah, from her father-in-law. The detailed narrative about Tamar, the story of her ardent loyalty in her widowhood, is based on the same *motif* as the romance of Ruth, and is, in its origin, not historical, but fictitious.

The same holds good regarding the *narrative about Dinah*, Jacob's daughter (Gen. xxxiv). There must have been an ancient historical tradition telling how the tribes Simeon and Levi attacked the town of Shechem in Central Palestine, and how the town was retained by the Canaanites. The other tribes of Israel rendered no help, and Simeon and Levi were dispersed and destroyed. This assumption is all the more justifiable because it is in entire agreement with what we learn from other sources regarding the subsequent fates of Simeon and Levi. Now legend has transformed these events in the

[1] Homer, *Il.* ix, ll. 447 ff Further references in my *Commentary on Genesis*.

JACOB

following fashion. It represents all the parties concerned, including Shechem, as young men. Both parties —and here we have the fictitious element coming in— begin to quarrel about a woman, the sister of Simeon and Levi, who has been loved and carried off by Shechem. In order to avenge this dishonour done to their sister, the two brothers took and killed the seducer, earning thereby their father's curse.

While in these cases the real basis of the legend is historical and the fictitious element is the addition, i.e. the legend has an historical core, it is, of course, possible to conceive the state of things reversed, so that folk-tale contributes the important parts and the historical names are a mere external attachment. This is the case in the *Joseph romance*. This narrative, given in great detail in our text both in J and E, deals in its essential parts with brethren who envy their youngest brother, a finer fellow than any of them, and determine to get him out of the way. At first the wicked plan succeeds. The poor lad becomes a miserable slave and is taken away to a distant land. But then the tables are turned. Owing to his abilities, he gains the high esteem of the king and attains an outstanding position. When, under the pressure of necessity, the wicked brethren betake themselves to the same country, they are delivered into the hands of the influential official, whom they do not recognize as their brother. But he does not pay them back in their own coin for the evil they had done him. There is a touching scene of recognition, in which he forgives and helps them. The expert will see at the first glance that this is a folk-tale, whose leading *motifs* are found again and again in the traditions of all nations. In fact, even many of the details, e.g. the boy with his predictive dreams which men vainly try to frustrate, his being thrown by his brethren into a well, occur in all versions of the story. This folk-tale was rendered suitable for use in Israel by receiving the addition that this youngest brother, the clever one, was the ancestor of the tribe of Joseph, and the other brothers were the fathers of the other tribes. In all this the only historical presupposition is that the tribe of Joseph was considered to be the youngest and best among the tribes. When the narrative was further expanded very little historical element was added. The essential parts of this narrative are thus derived from folk-tale.

Finally, something should be said as to how the statement originated that all these tribes and peoples were each derived from an ancestor, whose names were supposed to be contained in the historical national names: e.g. the tribe Joseph claims to be derived from a man of that name, and therefore calls itself "the sons of Joseph." This fundamental statement rests to some extent, as can be proved by many examples, especially among the Arabs and Turks, on a certain view of history. There are tribes which have been formed by a large and ever-increasing number of people attaching themselves to the family of an old sheik. Of course, the actual memory of this inherited or adopted ancestry has in most cases faded in course of time, so that nothing but the historical name was left. It is intelligible enough that the nation at a later time occupied itself with the question, "Who really was this man whose name is continually in everyone's mouth?" and the story-tellers gladly seized the opportunity of filling up this gap in the tradition. We have, then, to think of such an origin for the ancestral figure when a people calls itself "the sons of so-and-so." That is e.g., the case with Israel and Judah, but not, by the way, with Abraham, for ancient Israel never called itself "sons of Abraham." Nor is it true of Jacob, because the historical narrative never uses the expression "sons of Jacob," but always "sons of Israel." The figure of Jacob, therefore, like that of Abraham, must go back to a different origin.

The narratives already dealt with represent "the top layer" of the Jacob stories. They are further connected with the rest of the Jacob cycle by the insertion in the Laban stories of a passage dealing with *the birth of the sons of Jacob* (Gen. xxix. 31 ff.). Therefore, as the composite narrative shows, this passage represents a later dovetailing, and was invented for this very purpose by the narrators, who intended to tell afterwards stories about these sons. The passage, therefore, is not based on ancient popular tradition, and the vague style of its narrative clearly reveals this. For example, it is very noticeable how large a portion of it consists of ingenious explanations of the names of Jacob's children.

4.

Another and a deeper layer consists of a few *local legends dealing with theophanies and holy places*. In our present text they are inserted into the Esau and Laban stories. On his way from Esau to Laban, Jacob reaches Bethel; on his return journey he touches at Mahanaim, Peniel, Shechem, and, according to E, he comes a second time to Bethel.

We have only one brief note about Mahanaim (Gen. xxxii. 2). There Jacob saw the march of an army of God's angels, and therefore called the place "camp of the hosts."

Other brief local traditions are mentioned regarding places in the vicinity of Shechem (Gen. xxxiii. 12-30; xxxv. 4, 8, 14). There Jacob is said to have buried images under a terebinth, and to have purchased a sacred enclosure, erected a stone, and called on "El, God of Israel." At the same time we are told that he buried at Bethel Rebecca's nurse under the oak of weeping, and set up a stone over her grave.

These are all local traditions which, in view of their form, should be called "notices" rather than legends, and in their original form they resemble the short "notices" which are still in circulation among the people in many parts of Germany. They are only very loosely connected with the composite story of Jacob, both in content and in form. The compilers of the sources have inserted them at suitable places in their narrative. They were able to do this because the framework of the Jacob story which they possessed told of journeys of Jacob in the course of which he could have touched at these places. In doing so, they have, as a rule, followed the plan of putting first the religious material and then adding Jacob's secular adventures connected with the place in question. The fact that this artificial expedient was adopted betrays that these materials were only added to the rest when the tradition was reduced to writing. There is a further indication that they were inserted at a later time and do not belong to the oldest narrative. This is specially clear in connection with the notice about the burial of Rebecca's nurse, who is suddenly introduced here without any germane connection with the story: for why should Jacob be carrying his mother's nurse about with him wherever he went?

How, then, may the idea have arisen of *transferring*

JACOB

these trifling incidents to the hero of the Esau-Laban stories? The feature common to them all is that they deal with holy or venerable places in Israel. They must have been attributed to Jacob at a period when the latter was looked upon as national ancestor. It was *due* to the ancestor that he should have founded these places, or at least given them their names. In the same way, Shechem, Bethel, Hebron, and Beersheba were attributed to Abraham; Beer-lahai-roi, the sacred place of the tribe of Ishmael, to Ishmael's mother; and a few places to Isaac. That this explanation is correct is also evident from the fact that the memorial stone at Shechem bears the name " El, God of Israel." We may perhaps assume that tradition in Israel at one time called the founder of this holy place " Israel." In any case, we get no light here on the figure of Jacob.

The case is the same with the more expanded narratives of the same group. There is, first, the Peniel story (Gen. xxxii. 23). Alone at night, on the bank of the Jabbok—so we learn apparently both from J and E—the national progenitor was without any cause attacked by an unknown one and fought with him in mortal combat without weapons. Despite severe injury, Jacob bravely maintained his ground. Then the adversary fell to pleading: "Let me go: the morning breaks." At the dawn of a new day the demons of the night had to disappear. The words revealed to Jacob that his foe was a spirit, one of the beings called *elohim*, and with great presence of mind he utilized the opportunity and forced his adversary to " bless "him (i.e. to pronounce over him a magic word) ere he allowed the spectre of the night to escape from his iron grasp.

This narrative has hardly anything in common with the other Jacob stories. In particular, the figure of the patriarch contained in it is entirely different. Here he is a brave hero, who does not quail in an awesome situation, victor over men and gods. In the other stories he is a clever deceiver. What a contradiction arises from the coalescence of these so different legends in one figure! The same man who has just fought so bravely against a more than human foe tries in the immediate sequel to escape the anger of his brother by large gifts and smooth words! With great confidence we may here again infer that it was only at a later period that this story came into this connection and that it had originally no reference to Jacob.

What was this narrative originally? It was merely a local tradition about some hero or other, about whose contest with a demon of the night a story was current at Peniel. This explanation is supported by the existence of numerous parallel stories of similar night contests with a demon, and which, as has recently been suggested, go back ultimately to the experience of a nightmare.

But why should this story have been connected with Jacob instead of with some other figure? It was done by someone who identified Jacob with Israel. This is clear from two ætiological features. The fact that the "sons of Israel" do not eat the sciatic nerve of an animal is said to be due to the fact that, in that struggle, the god struck Jacob on the thigh; that is to say, a food custom peculiar to the Israelites is explained from an experience of their ancestor. Again, the change of name from Jacob to Israel is mentioned in the story. He who formerly was called Jacob is henceforth to be called Israel, i.e. striver with God, for, so says the god, he has "striven with gods and men." Here again it is natural to suppose that this story was told with reference to, and in explanation of, the name "Israel."

JACOB

Finally, there is the Bethel story (Gen. xxviii. 14 ff.). In Bethel, Jacob happens to sleep on a spot, afterwards sacred—to the Israel of history Bethel was a specially venerated sanctuary—sees there, according to E, a ladder stretching from heaven to earth, sets up as a memorial the stone on which he has rested, anoints it, names the place, and vows to offer there his tithes.

Like the preceding story, this one also ascribes to Jacob the foundation of a holy place, i.e. a local tradition is again transferred to him as Israel, father and founder of the holy places of his nation.

This narrative, handed down from old tradition, was now interwoven by the compilers of the Genesis sources with the Esau-Laban cycle. Jacob passes the place on his way from Esau to Laban and makes a vow, to be fulfilled if God will graciously guide him and bring him home. That is according to E. According to J, God promises him this of His own accord, and adds the promise to bestow on his posterity the land on which he was now encamped. Here, therefore, the present connection of the narrative within the composite story has been utilized to fill out with richer content the somewhat bare and scanty Bethel tradition.

Here again it is clear that compilers are at work, but the attainment of congruity in the character of Jacob, who has just, in disgraceful fashion, deceived his father and brother, and who now approaches God with a pious vow and is even abundantly blessed by Him, is not successful. These compilers, morally and artistically great, have tried to knit the whole structure more firmly together, and in so doing were naïve enough to introduce their own pious thoughts, but they were also undiscerning enough not to see how unsuitable a representative of these ideas the rascal Jacob really was. To produce a consistent picture they would have had to suppress or completely recast some of the stories. But they had not courage enough for that. A similar verdict must be passed upon the beautiful prayer of Jacob (Gen. xxxii. 10-13), which was probably inserted by a still later hand, before the meeting of Jacob and Esau, and which is equally out of keeping with the rest of the picture of Jacob. The later date of these features of the Bethel story is also proved by the fact that J conceives Jacob as the ancestor of Israel. It is to him and to his seed that the land is promised.

Thus far we have examined two of the strata of the Jacob narratives, the tales of the tribes of Israel and the local tales of holy places and theophanies. Both have been ascribed to Jacob under the presupposition that he is identical with Israel, the ancestor of the nation and the founder of its holy places. The writer of J shows a delicate perception when, in the later passages of his narrative—from Peniel onwards—he uses "Israel" instead of "Jacob." In neither of these layers have we found the real kernel of the Jacob stories.

5.

The case is quite different with the two deeper layers which treat of Jacob's relations to Esau and to Laban. Together, these narratives constitute a beautifully finished cycle of tales. It consists of three parts:

1. Jacob-Esau stories, Part I (Gen. xxv. 21 to xxvii).
2. Jacob-Laban stories (Gen. xxix. 15 to xxxii. 1).
3. Jacob-Esau stories, Part II (Gen. xxxii. 4 to xxxiii. 17).

That is to say, the narrators have given the Esau narrative in two portions and inserted the Laban tradition between them. Evidently that was done for the sake of the fine artistic impression produced by such a whole. The conclusion brings us back to the starting-point. The connecting link between the two is, as we have seen, Jacob's journeys. As we shall see afterwards, this *motif* has been taken from the Laban story. Further, the narrators have sought by all kinds of cross-references to attain a still closer unity. Hence Rebecca, Jacob's mother, must advise her son to flee to Laban, and when he arrives there Jacob has to tell Laban all that has happened. The two threads of narrative have been further assimilated by the invention of a relationship between the figures in the two strands. The mother of the deceiver in the Esau story is the sister of the deceived Laban. In spirit also the two strands have been brought into unity. In the earlier form of the narrative the questionable behaviour of Jacob is recounted with complacency, but later hands have toned down this original note and have added religious considerations, as far as that was possible—a procedure in which they have been surpassed by Bible expositors, both Jewish and Christian, down to the present day. Further, a romantic turn has been given to most of the separate stories, but this has not been carried out so fully here as in, say, the Joseph story. The original separate tales have not, however, been brought into complete agreement, and some ragged edges have been left. That Jacob, in his flight from Laban, is bound to fall into Esau's hands, neither Jacob nor the narrator himself sees; it is only after Laban has left Jacob that this new danger occurs to Jacob and to the narrator.

Our first task is to compare together *the first and*

second parts of the Esau narratives. The second part claims to be the continuation of the first. At the outset Esau is highly enraged by Jacob's deceit and is still full of wrath against his brother; but Jacob, returning from his sojourn with Laban, has to enter Esau's territory. How will he fare there? The continuation has not maintained complete consistency with the presuppositions of the first part. As we shall show in detail, the *motif* of the former narrative is the contest between the shepherd and the hunter. Jacob, the shepherd, wins the blessing from Esau the hunter. When the brothers meet again later, Jacob is still the shepherd, but Esau is now no longer a solitary hunter. He has become the leader of a band, gaining his livelihood in the desert at the head of four hundred men, and all that is left of the main *motif* of the earlier story, viz. the contest between the two, is that Jacob once more outwits Esau by his wiliness. So the *motif* or plot of this second part is: How is this astute shepherd, Jacob, accompanied by a large family and encumbered with numerous flocks of sheep and goats, to escape successfully in spite of all these impedimenta from this robber captain, who is so angry with him on account of his former trickery? The second part is therefore a later invention, not completely unified with the first. But the reason for the invention of such a sequel is clear. This old tale was so beautiful and so popular that there *had* to be a sequel. The listeners insisted on hearing more about Jacob and Esau, and the skilful story-tellers complied with this demand all the more readily as it gave them an opportunity of supplying a fine frame for the Laban story. Parallels to this kind of after-invention are abundant in literature. In the Old Testament itself we have a similar second part of the Samson-Delilah story, and a similar continuation of the story of the Shunammite woman (2 Kings iv. 1-6).

But the content of the story itself is the best proof that this is how it arose. It is well known that " sequels " of this kind rarely reach the level of the first production. Here, too, the sequel is inferior both in freshness and in power to the first part. Further, consider the localities of the stories. The scene of the first part is somewhere in the south of Canaan. Little importance attaches to the exact whereabouts; the only important thing is that shepherds and hunters live together there. But the second part takes place in an entirely different country, east of Jordan, in Mahanaim and Peniel. It is easy to see why this portion of the story must be located there. The scene is laid there because Jacob is there at the close of the Laban story, and this proves that the second part of the Esau narrative presupposes the preceding Laban tale. It was meant from the beginning to be the conclusion of the complete composite Esau-Laban narrative. We are told of the clever ruse by which Jacob here outwitted his brother. In Mahanaim he divided his flocks and servants into two camps. If Esau should attack the one, probably the other will be able to escape. He arranges his family in such a way that those least dear to him are put first, so that at least Rachel and Jacob in the rear may be able to flee. He sends on in front a large flock as a present for Esau, subdividing this flock again into five parts in order to make it appear more imposing. In all these " dividings " we have an echo of the name of the place where this is said to have happened, Mahanaim, " two camps," or " several camps." And there is also a play on words: *mahane*, " camp," and *minha*, " present." Thus no small part of the narrative is drawn from the name of the place, while other *motifs* are borrowed from the name " Peniel " and the word " Ford of Peniel " (see *Commentary on Genesis*, 3rd–5th ed., p. 355 ff.). The result is that the story has been built upon an imaginative interpretation of the names, like that which we have seen to be the case in the story of the birth of the children of Jacob. This is a further proof that we have here, not an ancient story independent of popular origin, but one which owes its existence to later narrators. Once more, *this* is not the soil out of which the Jacob figure arose.

6.

There now remain only the *Jacob-Esau stories, Part I*, and the *Jacob-Laban stories*. These are the real kernel of the whole composite Jacob narrative.[1] Here we have two very ancient folk-tales, dovetailed into each other at a later time. We must first try as far as we can to get at their oldest meaning.

The Jacob-Laban narrative is made up of the strands of several separate stories. The preface is a brief narrative, relating "*How Jacob comes to Laban*" (Gen. xxi. 1–14). The first member of that family that he sees is Rachel, afterwards so dear to him. He gains her favour and that of her father by taking her part against the other shepherds and watering her flocks for her. Exactly similar details are narrated about Moses, who in the same way gains the love of Zipporah and a friendly reception from her father. The story is therefore in no way specially characteristic of Jacob. Tales like these are " fatherless " and are

[1] I am flattered by the support of Gressmann and Kittel in this opinion. See *History of the People of Israel*, vol. i, 2nd ed., p. 753.

easily transferred from one person to another, just as the clouds on the mountains detach themselves from one peak to gather round another.

All the more significant for our purpose, therefore, are the ensuing stories (Gen. xxx. 25 to xxxii. 1) which have been blended into a splendid unit. They treat of *the game of " diamond cut diamond" between Jacob and Laban*. The former, who seems to have a very lucky hand in things pertaining to shepherd work, and who is therefore of great value to the rich flockmaster Laban, is tricked by the latter to serve him fourteen years without pay. Jacob has fallen in love with the fair Rachel and willingly serves her father seven years in order to win her. But when the time for the marriage comes he is put off with the less comely Leah and must serve another seven years for Rachel. Thus far Laban has tricked Jacob very badly. Now, however, he has his revenge. During the ensuing six years Jacob contrives by all manner of artifices to get into his possession a large part of Laban's flocks, and is even clever enough to escape from Laban with all his family and all his rich possessions, awkward to handle as these are. No doubt the oldest form of the tale gave all this with broad humour, thoroughly pleased with the way in which the cunning Laban was paid back with compound interest. A later time, feeling somewhat uncomfortable about these doings, although their morality could hardly be impeached, tried to retell the story as indulgently as possible for Jacob, and to show how justifiable his conduct was. Jacob is Laban's *son-in-law*. The two have a dispute about their shares—as fathers and sons-in-law may often do. The popular version is decisively on the young man's side. At first, it is true, the older man is the more astute ; but in the end the young man has learned something and outwits the older man pretty thoroughly. At this stage the narrative is altogether a splendid specimen of the racy, popular tale. That type of story delights in the theme of "diamond cut diamond," and loves to give the young man the advantage over the elder.[1]

Jacob and Laban are *shepherds*. Evidently the people amongst whom the stories were current were themselves shepherds, and what we have here are shepherds' tales. Laban is a Syrian (Aramean). As we have already shown, this proves that Jacob and Laban were not originally related to each other; in fact, they belong to different peoples. This feature also, viz. that men of different race are shown disputing or bargaining together, is a frequent subject in popular tale. In the Old Testament we find Joseph opposed to the lewd Egyptian woman. The *Thousand and One Nights* tell of "the faithful" in grips with Jews, Christians, and negroes, and the German tale is fond of introducing the Jew. And when Laban is specifically called an Aramean the presupposition is that the Aramean shepherds lived not very far distant from the Hebrew shepherds and that they were considered to be specially astute and deceitful. The reason for Jacob coming into touch with these foreigners is stated as being because he was obliged to leave his home country and to seek refuge in another land. A young man away from home gaining a girl's love and cleverly surmounting all the difficulties that her father puts in his way is found again and again in the folk-tale. This, therefore, is the original place for the *motif* that is used as connecting link in the Esau-Laban cycle, viz. that Jacob is on his travels.

The *scene of this tale* is, according to J, the large

[1] Cf. my *Märchen im Alten Testament*, p. 121.

city of Haran in Mesopotamia, but in the narrative itself there is no mention of such a populous place. On the contrary, the narrative presupposes an extensive pasture-land, on which the flocks may feed, sometimes days' journeys distant from each other. The original form is found in E, which speaks of the "East country." Ed. Meyer [1] has identified this with the great steppe to the east of Damascus. From this localization we can read the entire history. Aramean sheep-breeders, we shall suppose, once pastured their flocks in the Syrian-North-Arabian steppe, till at a later period they made their way into Mesopotamia and made Haran their capital. The Laban tale followed them thither. Originally, however, Jacob was a guest among the Arameans of the "East land," the most distant point between them and the Hebrews being Mispah, on the east of Jordan.

At the close of the tale, according to E, a treaty was made between Laban and Jacob. With great reluctance Laban had to let Jacob go, taking his family and his flocks with him, but he exacted from him the promise not to wrong his daughters by marrying other wives.

In J the story is different. According to this account the treaty made on this occasion was of historical and national importance. Jacob and Laban mutually agreed upon a frontier that was not to be crossed by either with hostile intent. Jacob stands here, therefore, for the people of Israel and Laban for the people of Aram, and the frontier fixed upon is that which the two nations are to respect. Now it is noteworthy that the idea that both men are national ancestors appears nowhere except in this one passage in the whole Laban story, and that only in J. Up till now both have been merely indi-

[1] Ed. Meyer, *Die Israeliten und ihre Nachbarstämme*, p. 243.

viduals, and although Laban is occasionally called "the Aramean," he is never called "the father of Aram." We conclude, therefore, that Jacob in these stories was originally a private individual, but was subsequently transformed into the ancestor of Israel. By this reminting, legendary and historical elements have been combined, just as in the tribal legends of the sons of Jacob with which we have already dealt. The latter narrative, in which historical matter has been added to what was originally a folk-tale, but in which the ancient material has been kept very clear and the added historical matter is very loosely attached, is an instructive parallel.

Therefore the original figure of Jacob in the Laban narrative is the figure of a shepherd, a very shrewd man, temporarily a guest amongst foreigners (Arameans), who marries there and outwits his astute father-in-law—altogether the very type of the hero of a folk-tale.

7.

We have now to compare this Jacob of the Laban stories with the Jacob of the *Esau tales* (Gen. xxv. 21 to xxviii. 22). Here again our first task is to get at *the oldest meaning of the narrative, and so get at the original figure of the hero*.

In this passage also our sources have put a national interpretation on the events—clearly in J, less clearly in E. In a brief passage prefixed to the whole we are told that the mother of Jacob and Esau, while the children were still unborn, was conscious of unusual happenings in her womb. In her trouble she consulted the oracle and received the answer:

JACOB

> Two nations bearest thou in thy womb,
> Two tribes separate from thy body;
> Tribe shall tribe o'erwhelm,
> The elder be slave to the younger.

At the end of the tale of Jacob's deception the blessing, which he extorts from his blind father, declares:

> Peoples shall serve thee
> And nations bow before thee.

The nations indicated here are clear. "Jacob" is, of course, Israel, and Esau means Edom. Esau is to bear the name Edom, i.e. "red man," because he exchanged his birthright for a mess of red pottage. In the story of the birth there are hints to the same effect: when Esau was born he was "red," and was, to the touch, like a hairy cloak. This last is a humorous reference to Edom's country Seir, the name of which resembles in sound the Hebrew word for "hair." This identification of Esau with Edom is also found elsewhere, especially in the genealogical lists given in Genesis xxxvi, where Esau is identified with Edom, or, according to another view, with Edom's father; also in the prophetic writings, where the Edomites are occasionally called "sons of Esau"; but Seir is undoubtedly the name of a Horite primitive people that occupied the country before Edom and was afterwards subdued and absorbed by it, so that Edom could also in poetical language be called by that name.

Now the Jacob-Esau stories told how Jacob defrauded his brother of *his birthright* and of *his father's blessing*. The word "birthright" is also used elsewhere in similar connections with reference to nations. The meaning is that the one people surpasses the kindred one in age, power, and wealth. And, similarly, the

" blessing " of which Jacob deprived his brother means the bestowal of the better country and the superior power. According to this view, therefore, the saga is supposed to mean that Edom, although it was in earlier days the more important people, has had to relinquish its power to Israel, which was previously inferior to it, and is, in fact, now under its dominion. We know enough of the history of both nations to understand the meaning of this—Edom is an older people than Israel. It abandoned nomadic life earlier than Israel and had a king at an earlier period than Israel. Subsequently Israel obtained the richer territory.

> So may God give thee
> Of the dew of heaven
> And of the rich fields of earth.

So we read in the " blessing of Jacob," and in the end Israel under David subdued Edom.

Thus the most natural supposition would be that the tale arose merely as a poetical representation of this national relationship. Against this, however, there are several weighty objections. First of all, the striking fact that in both cases two names are used for one figure suggests that the process was not an entirely simple one. Jacob and Israel on the one hand, and Esau and Edom on the other hand, cannot surely be the same, seeing that they bear different names. Besides, the tale speaks, not of Israel and Edom, but of Jacob and Esau, whereas, *vice versa*, the historical accounts never speak of Jacob and Esau, but always only of Israel and Edom. This leads us to conclude that the figures in the tale arose in some other way, and were transferred to the two tribes only in later tradition. Again, in the narratives there is very little mention indeed of these peoples or of national relationships. Apart from the hints and allusions at the end and at the beginning of the narratives, the actors make throughout the impression of actual individuals. It is specially noteworthy that, when they are looked at more closely, these stories do not at all fit Israel and Edom. In the folk-tale Jacob is, to be sure, astute, but there is little bravery about him. When his brother is angry with him, he flees. He obtains the birthright entirely by means of superior cunning, but in the historical accounts Israel overcame Edom by force of arms, and fierce Joab, David's commander, who subdued Edom, would hardly have felt honoured by being likened to wily Jacob. The same is true of the figure of Esau. In the folk-tale his chief quality is thoughtlessness or guilelessness. He allows himself to be overreached ; but in the historical accounts, as various Biblical references show,[1] Edom was specially renowned just for its sagacity and wisdom. In the folk-tale the two brothers are shepherd and hunter ; but there is no proof that these were the chief occupations of the two peoples in the historical times when they lived side by side.

We have many reasons, therefore, for the supposition that it was later redactors who gave these stories a new interpretation with a reference to national relationships, and that the narratives had originally a quite different meaning. This supposition will seem less difficult when we remember that exactly the same is true of Jacob's adventures with Laban. We must, therefore, try to read the Esau stories without this new turn that has been given to them. What would then be their meaning ?

The main root of the narratives consists of two folk-tales, both of which tell *how the precedence passed from*

[1] See my *Commentary on Genesis*, 3rd- 5th eds., p. 316.

Esau to Jacob, i.e. they both deal with what is really one theme, although, according to one version, this took place by purchase, and, according to the other, by deception. Both are at one also in the statement that the two are brothers—an interjected introduction calls them twin brothers; also that they differ in calling and in natural gifts. *Jacob is shepherd, Esau is hunter. In all their main features the narratives are based on this difference of calling between the two.*

The first saga tells how Esau comes home from the chase starving with hunger. He has—so it is understood—caught nothing that day, and is ready to devour what he can find. Jacob, however, who had remained comfortably at home, has something to eat even to-day. He has prepared for himself a tasty soup—the implication is that, although he was a shepherd, he also did some field work. Thus the foolish Esau makes over his birthright to Jacob for a " mess of pottage."

This narrative sets in contrast types of two different occupations—a very frequent subject of folk-tale. In German folk-tale we find brought thus together farmer and woodcutter, cobbler and tailor, shepherd boy and king's daughter. It is also a familiar feature of this kind of tale that the representatives of the callings are *brothers*. " A certain man had two sons: the one was a cobbler, the other a smith." That is a typical opening of a German folk-tale. Hebrew saga knows also of two brothers—Abel, a shepherd, and Cain, a tiller of the ground. Another tradition, almost entirely lost, told of three brothers, Jabal, a shepherd, Jubal, a musician, and Tubal, a smith. That the different actors are conceived as brothers is explained by the fact that the relationship of brother is one of the simplest family relationships, just the type that primitive narrative is

JACOB

able to conceive and handle. The regular *motif* of such 'tales of calling" is that the one claims to be superior to the other. Such stories would be told where representatives of the callings lived together and one was keen to magnify its importance and its superiority over the other. In the German Märchen the point usually is, " Who is to win the bride ? " Abel and Cain dispute as to whose sacrifice is to gain God's favour. Here Jacob and Esau dispute about the "birthright." This, it is to be understood, carries with it the whole inheritance left by the father and the dominion over the other. Admittedly it belongs by right to the hunter, but the shepherd has purchased it from him. Such a tale can only have arisen in a country in which shepherds and hunters dwelt together, as is still the case, for example, among the Targi in the Sahara, among the Masai, Abyssinians, etc. Those who tell each other stories of this kind are shepherds themselves, and they relate with pride and glee how the hunter, although he was the first-born and his calling was considered the superior one, had to take an inferior place behind the shepherd. That the calling of the hunter is considered the superior occupation is also found elsewhere. The Targi are divided into the nobility, who carry on hunting, war, and robbery, and the shepherd class, which ranks below these. In its naïve way, the tale has given the historical process by which the hunter gave way before the shepherd, but it also reveals splendid powers of detailed observation. The hunter's only skill is that of knowing how to kill the animal that comes into his power. He lives, therefore, from hand to mouth. If he comes home some day empty-handed, he must just go hungry. But as long as he has something to eat to-day he does not trouble about to-morrow. " Esau ate and drank, rose up and went forth, having thrown away his birthright." On the other hand, the shepherd is a man of a different type. "While the hunter remains an impecunious man, who needs to find his living day by day, the shepherd is to some extent a capitalist, living on his interest."[1] He does not kill the animals in his care, but draws daily profit from them. He has food every day, and wisely thinks not only of to-day, but also of the morrow. Thus Jacob the shepherd proves superior to the hunter Esau. The whole narrative is thus to be understood as a folk-tale dealing with men of different callings.

In the related narrative of *Jacob's deception* the same *motif* undergoes another twist. In this tale, the thing that belongs of right to Esau, and which Jacob desires, is the father's *blessing*. The blessing, i.e., occupies here the place held by the birthright in the other story. There is a simple philological explanation of this interchange. *Bekora*, "birthright," and *Beraka*, "blessing," have a phonetic resemblance. Such plays on words were always popular in Israel. Moreover, the blessing in question implies a precedence of the one over the other. It implies the better inheritance and dominion over the brother, i.e. in effect it amounts to the same thing as the birthright. In form, such a blessing is a magic word. When once it has been pronounced it cannot be recalled. And the old man cannot utter it till after he has "strengthened his soul" by a good meal. The dying father is anxious to give this blessing to his first-born. He loves him, for—as it is naïvely put—he loves the venison he provides. So he sends him afield to secure this dainty for him. The mother,

[1] R. Hildebrand, *Law and Custom at the More Primitive Economic Stages*, 2nd ed., p. 24.

who prefers her quiet son Jacob, has overheard the conversation and secures the blessing for her own favourite by killing two kids and tying their skins round his neck and arms. To the touch he is exactly like his brother. Thus E. In J, the ruse by which Isaac is deceived is even more subtle. Jacob puts on his brother's best clothes, and these have their owner's characteristic odour.

This story also is completely on the level of the folk-tale, where the same plot is frequently met with, how the clever but weak one outwits the strong but stupid one, and where there is a special fondness for the childish, roguish exchange of clothes. There are tales in which the prince puts on a sheep's stomach over his curls and is then taken by everyone for a bald person. There is the tale of the disguises of the wolf in Grimm's tale of "the seven young kids." As A. Thimme says in his book *Das Märchen* (p. 56): "In the tale there is no feeling of moral indignation at such roguery, because laughter over the success of the trick displaces all moral resentment."

Our tale shows representatives of two callings in conflict, and the shepherd supplants the hunter. The latter is pictured as belonging to a rough type of humanity—he is as hairy as a kid and his odour is so strong that it is even perceptible in his new clothes. On the other hand, the shepherd is more civilized. He is smooth of skin and attaches more value to personal cleanliness. The hunter roams about out of doors and is his father's favourite; but the mother loves best the quiet Jacob, who stays about the house. The hunter's venison tastes better than the tame meat provided by the shepherd, but the art of cookery is already able to conceal such differences. The hunter is a violent man—

Esau means to kill his brother; but the shepherd does not deal in violence, he avoids the open crime, but he is clever and reaches his goal by trickery.

In view of all this, there can be no further doubt in any mind that the Esau stories are really examples of tales of callings, with a plot of shepherd *versus* hunter, and that the ethnological colour of the narrative was added at a later stage. In all these compositions we see the same principle at work—we are dealing with ancient folk-tales interwoven with historical reminiscences.

In the Laban stories the plot is similar. They deal with the young astute shepherd and his successful contest of wits against a man who is really his superior. It is easy to understand how the two similar cycles of stories attracted each other and were referred to the same person. But when we compare them in respect of originality, there can be no hesitation. The Laban stories do not, like the Esau stories, bear the mark of great antiquity and of distinct individuality. They rather belong to the " fatherless " tales, which can easily be fathered on another person. This finds confirmation in the arrangement of the composite narrative, which places the Esau stories first and the Laban stories at the end.[1]

8.

Our conclusion, therefore, is: *The Esau stories are the real kernel of the Jacob tradition.* Jacob is originally the type of the shepherd who ousts the hunter. With reference to the name Jacob, it is simply a proper name of that period, such as the heroes of German folk-tales

---

[1] In this I have the support of Gressmann See also Kittel, *History of the People of Israel*, p. 34, note 2.

JACOB

also bear. We find it as such in Babylonian literature. The name Jacob (Jaqubum) is abbreviated from Jacob-el (Jahqub-il, Jaqub-il), and it occurs in the time of Hammurabi. That it was also known in the West we learn from the list of Thutmosis III (*circa* 1500 B.C.), where it appears as the name of a Canaanite town. Names of similar formation in Canaan are also to be found in the Tell-el-Amarna period.[1] Thus it is not surprising to find this same name in an ancient Hebrew folk-tale. The objection—raised more than once in recent years—that Jacob was not a Canaanite name, has little force, for, after all, we know practically nothing of the names from that primitive time. And why should the folk-tale be confined to the commonest names ? Regarding the name Esau we can say nothing at all. Whether it is in any way connected with the Phœnician Usoos, the hunter and the enemy of the brother Samemrumos, must be left an open question.

The subsequent history of the Jacob figure was probably as follows :

First of all, to Jacob, who outwitted Esau, was referred a second story, which dealt likewise with a young, clever shepherd. In this way the *Laban story* was added.

Simultaneously, a continuation was invented for the Esau story, i.e. what we have called Part II of the Esau story arose.

The biggest step, however, was taken when Jacob was declared to be the ancestor of Israel. At that period a new meaning was given to the older tales— Esau was identified with Edom and Laban with Aram. At the same time the name Jacob was inserted into a whole series of other tales which dealt with the tribes and with the holy places of Israel. The complete figure

[1] Kittel, *op. cit.*, i, p. 417, note 2.

thus arose by the addition of the Israel tradition to the Jacob tradition.

It is also possible to give some indication of the time when this process took place. The new interpretation introducing Esau dates from the time subsequent to the conquest of Edom by David (after 980). The addition to the Blessing (Gen. xxvii. 40) seems to indicate that Edom afterwards threw off the yoke of Israel (840). The same period is indicated by the Laban stories, because in the boundary treaty with him not a word is said about the Syrian wars (860–770). That the Syrians would one day break out in rage against Israel and dismember it, the redactor did not dream. The introduction of the political reference, therefore, dates from the time of the early kingdom in Israel. But the original Jacob story must be much older. It must come from the primitive age of Israel, when the people consisted of shepherds and hunters. Another consideration leads us to fix the same date. When Israel, after its unification under the first kings, began to be again conscious of its unity, it began to ask about its ancestors, and chose as these the most popular figures that its traditions provided.

The compelling motive of this growth and transformation of the Jacob figure is quite plain. It is clear that the people loved this figure. In it ancient Israel with joy recognized itself, so it selected him as its ancestor. Of course that is a popularity which we cannot see without some regret. But we must remember that the Germans take pleasure in Baron Münchausen, and that the Hellenes saw in Odysseus a popular hero, if not an ancestor. Above all, we must remember that, alongside of Jacob, Israel chose for ancestor another and a nobler figure—viz. Abraham.

INDEX

Artistic qualities of O.T., 19

Books of the O.T., growth of, 63

Christianity and O.T., 34 ff.
Criticism, results of, 14

Dirge, the, 65
Dirge, Individual, 80 f., 98
Dirge, National, 80 f.

Eschatology in O.T., 40

Freiligrath, 32

God in O.T., 45, 49
    His aloofness, 102

Hebrew music, 27
Hebrew religion, 33
Hindrances to the understanding of O.T., 16
History in O.T., 30
Hymns, 72 ff.

" I " of the Psalms, 118
Immortality in the Psalter, 105
Individual religion in O.T., 93
Inspiration, 18 f.

Jacob, real kernel of the narratives, 172 f.
Job, Book of, 19, 29

Literary history of O.T., 58
Lyrical poetry of O.T., 25

Monotheism, 38
Morality in O.T., 15, 39

Nature in O.T., 41

Old Testament as children's book, 20, 31 f.
Old Testament in the Church, 13, 34

Patriarchal figures, 150 f.
Personality, wealth of, 52
Poetical narratives of O.T., 20
Politics and religion, 42
Psalms, classified, 72 f.
    Royal, 88

Religion and Politics, 42
Religious value of O.T., 33
Retribution, doctrine of, 38

Suffering, 105

Teachers and the O.T., 17, 54
Types, literary, 59 ff.

Units, brevity of, 62 f.

World history, idea of, 43

www.ingramcontent.com/pod-product-compliance
Lightning Source LLC
Chambersburg PA
CBHW050806160426
43192CB00010B/1662